AWAY on BUSINESS

AWAY on BUSINESS

◆

THE HUMAN SIDE OF CORPORATE TRAVEL

Gunna Dickson

iUniverse, Inc.
New York Lincoln Shanghai

AWAY on BUSINESS
THE HUMAN SIDE OF CORPORATE TRAVEL

Copyright © 2007 by Reuters

All rights reserved. No part of this book may be used or reproduced by any means, graphic, electronic, or mechanical, including photocopying, recording, taping or by any information storage retrieval system without the written permission of the publisher except in the case of brief quotations embodied in critical articles and reviews.

iUniverse books may be ordered through booksellers or by contacting:

iUniverse
2021 Pine Lake Road, Suite 100
Lincoln, NE 68512
www.iuniverse.com
1-800-Authors (1-800-288-4677)

The views expressed in this work are solely those of the author and do not necessarily reflect the views of the publisher, and the publisher hereby disclaims any responsibility for them.

ISBN-13: 978-0-595-42378-1 (pbk)
ISBN-13: 978-0-595-86714-1 (ebk)
ISBN-10: 0-595-42378-7 (pbk)
ISBN-10: 0-595-86714-6 (ebk)

Printed in the United States of America

Contents

Introduction ix

Part I IMAGE

CHAPTER 1   One Strike, and You're Out! 3
CHAPTER 2   All the World's a Corporate Stage 6
CHAPTER 3   Life Is a Cabernet 9
CHAPTER 4   Humor Is No Laughing Matter 12
CHAPTER 5   The Well-Dressed Traveler 15
CHAPTER 6   When Good Travelers Go Bad 17
CHAPTER 7   Deals on Wheels 20
CHAPTER 8   Breaking the Language Barrier Overseas 23

Part II RELATIONSHIPS

CHAPTER 9   Absence Makes a Spouse Grow Sadder 27
CHAPTER 10   Emotional Tradeoff for Traveling Moms 30
CHAPTER 11   The Road Test for Fidelity 33
CHAPTER 12   Friends Behind Bars 36
CHAPTER 13   Traveling With, or Without, Your Best Friend .. 39
CHAPTER 14   In the Corporate Trenches 42

Part III HEALTH

CHAPTER 15	Don't Worry, Be Happy	47
CHAPTER 16	Making the Most of a Working Breakfast	50
CHAPTER 17	Staying in the Comfort Zone	53
CHAPTER 18	Soaking Up Serenity	56
CHAPTER 19	When Work Is Done, a Play's the Thing	59
CHAPTER 20	Illness and Theft are Occupational Hazards	61
CHAPTER 21	Environment Control	64

Part IV AIR TIME

CHAPTER 22	Sky-Level Gourmet Dining	69
CHAPTER 23	Sky's the Limit for In-Flight Magazines	72
CHAPTER 24	Airport Hotels Get Image Makeover	75
CHAPTER 25	Seat-Pocket Gift-Shopping	78
CHAPTER 26	Life after Concorde	81

Part V HOTELS

CHAPTER 27	Kept Awake by Bells and Whistles?	87
CHAPTER 28	Recipe for Success	91
CHAPTER 29	Strange Bedfellows	94
CHAPTER 30	Expanding Your Horizons	97
CHAPTER 31	When Guests Speak, Hotels Listen	100
CHAPTER 32	Vying for Rooms With Donkeys and Elephants	103
CHAPTER 33	It's Beginning to Look a Lot Like Christmas	106

Part VI	**SEPTEMBER 11, 2001**	
CHAPTER 34	Taking It One Step at a Time	111
CHAPTER 35	De-Accessorizing Long Flights	114
CHAPTER 36	Air Travelers Look to the Heavens	117
CHAPTER 37	Corporate Bookings Reflect 9-11	120
Part VII	**WAR**	
CHAPTER 38	Another Battle in the War on Stress	125
CHAPTER 39	For Concierge, it's Business as Usual	128
CHAPTER 40	Insurance in the Face of Danger	131
CHAPTER 41	Drawing Up a Corporate Battle Plan	134
CHAPTER 42	Keeping Their Eyes on the Prize	137
CHAPTER 43	Tense Times Put Bosses on Front Lines	140
CHAPTER 44	Survival of the Fittest	143
Part VIII	**TRAVEL TRENDS**	
CHAPTER 45	Charity begins at work	149
CHAPTER 46	A Woman's Changing World	152
CHAPTER 47	An Alternative Point of View	155
CHAPTER 48	The Expatriate Life	158
CHAPTER 49	Middle East Meets West	161
CHAPTER 50	Making a World of Difference	164
CHAPTER 51	Meeting of Minds on the Seas	167
CHAPTER 52	Onward and Upward	170

Part IX TIME OUT

CHAPTER 53 A World of Opportunities 175

CHAPTER 54 Navigating the Euro Zone 178

CHAPTER 55 Armchair Travel for Idle Dynamos 181

About the Author 185

Introduction

Much is written about the latest technological developments and strategies for success to give business travelers an edge over their competition.

But, in the end, success may be measured as much by what happens before or after a meeting, as during the actual session. It is driven by the people who take part.

This collection of columns looks at the human side of corporate travel, the issues affecting individuals who wrestle with motivation, safety, stress, education and down-time management issues while dealing with concerns about leaving a spouse, children or pets behind as they circle the globe for their companies.

The information within these columns comes from people who are experts in their fields–doctors, hotel and airline executives, financial and military analysts, motivational speakers, chefs, authors, parents and seasoned road warriors.

I am grateful to these valuable and valued sources for sharing their expertise. They have helped to make this book an evergreen and entertaining source of information.

—Gunna Dickson

PART I
IMAGE

1

One Strike, and You're Out!

You have 10 seconds; no more than 90. That's how long it takes to form a first impression, which for business travelers can ultimately sink or seal a deal.

"The first 10 seconds is enough to establish like or dislike," says Patti Wood, body language expert and public speaker based in Atlanta. "The first critical minute—the ritual of Hello! What's your name? Where are you from?—is tribal. It establishes the safety and comfort level between individuals."

In other words, the more you have in common, the more quickly a bond might be formed.

But even if you're worlds apart, all is not lost.

"Do your research; it's important," Wood said. "In other countries, business executives might go to two weeks of classes in etiquette, eating and gift giving. Imagine you're doing business with someone who has been educated about you. You need to do the same thing."

In business, the basic components of a good first impression are attire suited to the occasion and appropriate demeanor.

What you wear at the first meeting—a business suit or sweater and slacks—says something about you and sets the tone. Regardless of how well prepared you are, if you're inappropriately dressed, even your best proposals may not have the desired effect for your company.

For maximum success in making a good business impression, you need to dress like the culture of the country you are visiting. For instance, a tie is not always required for businessmen in Brazil, but manicured nails for women are considered important. Arms and legs should be kept covered in Muslim countries, and good shoes are a must in France.

"Different outfits are appropriate for different occasions. Consider your attire as a costume for playing your part," says the Mannersmith Monthly newsletter from Mannersmith, an etiquette consulting firm that creates seminars for clients, from children to CEOs (http://www.mannersmith.com).

If you have any doubts, before you travel, consult an international traveler's guide such as Getting Through Customs (http://www.getcustoms.com), which produces international Web-based products, conducts seminars and employs the authors of best-selling international business books. Electronic products include: "Kiss, Bow or Shake Hands: How to Do Business in Sixty Countries;" "Dun & Bradstreet's Guide to Doing Business Around the World," and the International Business Traveler's Series for Latin America and the European Union.

World traveler and international businessman Guenter J. Hude, general manager for the Americas at Austrian Airlines (www.aua.com), makes an important distinction for traveling business executives: Their attire is often dictated by the distance they must cover.

"Within Europe, business-class passengers tend to be very smartly dressed, but there's a good reason. The flight is usually brief and they are going straight to a meeting," said Hude from his office in Whitestone, New York.

"Long-haul business passengers, on the other hand, might arrive for check-in wearing blue jeans and running shoes because they need to be comfortable," he added. "But regardless of what they're wearing, the byword for our in-flight staff is 'verwoehnen,' which means to pamper someone as you would a guest in your own home."

As for demeanor, says Hude, "Our staff have observed that the more important a job the passenger has, the easier they make it for the attendants. They have nothing to prove. The ones who make the most demands are usually the ones whose jobs are not quite as important—the nouveau riche of travel."

Attire and demeanor aside, putting on your best game face is crucial to making a good impression in any corporate presentation. To do that, some top businessmen are turning to something that women have used all along—makeup.

"Our face is what we put forward every day." said Nicole Tracy Lindenbaum, co-founder of Los Angeles-based La Bella Donna cosmetics and its Minerals for Men line. "Appearance is key. Women have always known it, but men are catching up."

"Men don't want to fuss, so this sheer covering feels like you have nothing on your face, yet it gives a healthy glow to all skin types and tones." (http://www.labelladonna.com).

When introducing their brand to the market, even established companies are not immune to the pressures of having to make a good first impression.

They have only one chance to get it right.

(February 2002)

"Reprinted with permission. All rights reserved. © Reuters 2002."

2

All the World's a Corporate Stage

In the footlights on the stage of world commerce, the communications skills of corporate travelers speak volumes for their companies.

On any given day, those skills may be called upon in the presentation of products and strategies, formal introductions, cocktail party small talk, or a congratulatory toast.

A speech overseas can be especially challenging because of cultural differences.

That form of communication readiness often takes more than a natural ability. It requires training and practice.

"When you're sitting on an airplane, you might write a really great speech," says executive and public speaking coach Reesa Woolf. "But the biggest mistake people make is that the first time they give it is in front of the real audience."

"It's important, like a Broadway actor, to rehearse the speech out loud three or four times. If you're pressed for time, rehearse the opening and the close," said Woolf, whose practice includes clients from "C-level executives" (CEOs, CFOs and COOs), to entrepreneurs who realize the importance of delivering information in a way that holds people's interest.

British media and public relations consultant Paul Smith, managing director of UK-based Paul Smith Associates, agrees that public speaking and show business have a lot in common.

"Speakers who lack entertainment value, can quickly lose an audience," said Smith, whose firm has handled publicity for major companies such as British-and U.S.-based eye surgery company LaserVision and LSG SkyChefs, the catering unit of German air carrier Deutsche Lufthansa with kitchens at airports around the world.

Smith's firm, located about an hour outside of London, also specializes in booking professional athletes to speak at major sporting events.

"The corporate side of sports is absolutely huge, whether it's football, horse racing or motor racing," said Smith, who books some of the world's leading jockeys to go into corporate hospitality areas at major racing venues such as Royal Ascot or the Aintree Grand National and talk to VIP guests about the racehorses, their chances of winning, and even offer a word of advice for first-time visitors to the track.

But like any other corporate presenters, the athletes are held to an international industry standard.

"As speakers, they must be entertaining, informative and knowledgeable," said Smith, who admits to drawing inspiration from some "very slick American speakers" at a major recruitment conference he attended in Las Vegas. "They know how to deliver the message and how to use props to their best advantage.

"If you're going to use video clips, you need to prepare, rehearse, and above all, make sure the technology works," Smith said, adding that he has seen very good speakers thrown off completely when their technical support system fails.

"Presentation skills rate up there with being technically capable," executive coach Woolf concurs. "Obviously, you have to know what you're doing on the job. But equally important, you have to be able to communicate that to your bosses and to your peers."

A major pitfall is not knowing your audience.

When a Midwestern publishing executive began his speech with "When my wife found out my company was moving to New York, she locked herself in the closet," his remarks were met with a stony silence. While that kind of unsophisticated regional humor may have played well in his hometown, the New York audience wasn't inclined to laugh.

If you're planning a presentation overseas, say in Tokyo or Shanghai, any problems that arise are likely to be compounded by cultural differences, said Woolf from her office in Boonton, New Jersey.

"Look for people in the U.S. who are of that culture and ask them to listen to your speech. Or call your contact in that country and try out a joke you are considering. If they laugh, then ask them if it would be appropriate for you to use it in a presentation," she said.

Speaking the same language, however, is no guarantee that things will go smoothly. Sometimes it is said, only half-jokingly, that the English and Americans are separated by a common language.

Among the many books offering guidance for doing business abroad, is a series by Roger E. Axtell of "Do's and Taboos Around the World" (John Wiley & Sons, Inc.), each tackling a different topic, such as "A Guide to International Behavior, 3rd edition," "Body Language Around the World" and "Using English Around the World", where an entire section—English: the Global Language—deals with what Americans need to know to be understood in other English-speaking nations such as Great Britain, Canada, Australia, New Zealand and South Africa.

A mistake commonly made is to misidentify the accents of the people in those countries—by asking a Scot, for instance, where in Australia he comes from.

Axtell writes: "Those who confuse a South African with an Australian or a New Zealander because of accent put themselves in a balls-up situation. (Read that as a 'messed up and embarrassing' situation.)"

Being embarrassed is something all speakers are desperate to avoid. Just standing up and talking in front of a group of people is scary enough.

The fear of public speaking is the No. 1 ranked phobia in the United States, affecting a reported 75 percent of Americans, who fear it more than spiders, or even death.

The anxiety-induced "deer-in-the-headlights" syndrome is said to be one of the greatest impediments to career mobility.

Ready to help are scores of organizations and Internet Web sites offering leadership skills and, among other things, ready-made speeches.

At http://www.Need-A-Speech.com, on the "Professional" link are previews for topics as specific as "For a company announcing a downsizing" to "When things are not going well and you are going to have to introduce new tactics or adopt a new approach" and "Celebrating a success on the road to even greater things!" As a career investment, a "Complete Pack Including A Great Speech" would appear to be a bargain for "Just $16."

(October 2002)

"Reprinted with permission. All rights reserved. © Reuters 2002."

3

Life Is a Cabernet

Executives caught in a social vortex of cocktail parties and dinners, restaurant wine lists and formal toasts, find that drinking is a big part of life on the road.

"There is tremendous pressure to indulge in alcohol on business-social occasions," says Fred Knapp, president and CEO of Frederick Knapp Associates Inc., New York-based providers of corporate leader development seminars. "It is a factor in building business relationships, or bonding."

"The most popular safe business-image libations are wine and scotch, challenged in the last decade by vodka mixed drinks. But a vodka Martini, because it is so potent, is a negative at high visibility times," said Knapp, who over 25 years has coached the CEOs of 31 corporations, diplomats and top-level managers from 29 countries. "Beer, if a client is drinking it, allows you to do the same ... but always order a premium or name brand."

Those who do not consume alcoholic beverages should have something that looks like one, or order a glass of wine and let it sit on the table, he advises. "At least be gracious to the point of ordering as part of the relationship-building process."

Certain other guidelines should be kept in mind.

"There is nothing inherently wrong with drinking," says Dr. Marc Galanter, a professor of psychiatry at NYU School of Medicine, specializing in treating alcohol and drug abuse. "Generally, you can metabolize one drink in an hour, so if you keep to that limit, you'll be able to maintain a reasonably sober state."

While business-related social drinking is the norm in many parts of the world, some countries ban alcohol or restrict its use.

With the exception of Saudi Arabia, Kuwait and Iran, alcohol is not illegal in Muslim countries in the Middle East, says Lin Todd, president of Washington-based Global Risk international security consultants.

"In Kuwait, alcohol is not legally available to business travelers, although it is served at diplomatic functions," said Todd, recently returned from Kuwait and

Iraq. He cautions travelers to be very careful not to bring alcohol in their luggage to a country that outlaws it.

Violators of the law risk arrest and prosecution.

Alcohol availability in Iraq depends on a variety of things, such as a specific location or restaurant patronage.

"In Baghdad, establishments will or will not serve alcohol in deference to their main customers. Those catering to local Arabs in religiously conservative neighborhoods will not, but for hotels that cater to foreign visitors or traveling executives, it is good business." said Todd, who has lived and worked in Syria, Saudi Arabia, Bahrain, Jordan, Egypt and Lebanon.

Frequent travelers anywhere should be wary: Sooner or later, out-of-towners will get ripped off in a bar. Some solid advice on avoiding "gyp-bars" can be found on page 33 of "The New American Bartender's Guide" (New American Library), by John J. Poister, president of General Strategics, Inc., a New York-based communications consulting company.

Poister, a world traveler and author of five books on food and wine, offers a number of tips on spotting ways that gyp-bars bilk clientele, including trick shot glasses, packing a glass with tiny cubes of "dice-ice," cheap off-brand liquor and "no-show" drinks.

"If a drink is warm, weak or watery, send it back," he says. "If you are paying for premium gin in your Martini, make sure you get it."

For executive training, customized FKA seminars (www.frederickjknappinc.com) have included Execu-Speak, Execu-Image, Execu-Style and Execu-Etiquette, addressing topics such as business lunch, cocktail hour, what to drink—when and why, how to propose a toast and how to order from the wine list.

"When choosing a bottle of wine in a restaurant, many people get tense because they don't feel they are connoisseurs. But they should not be embarrassed to ask the wine steward to assist them," Knapp said. He recommends the wine list's mid-to-upper range, the range from which stewards often select. Above middle price point is also a logical area, he adds.

Formal toasts are often given between courses. Instead of clinking the glass, however, it is better simply to rise and say: "May I have your attention, please," Knapp said.

A quick guide to international toasts is the Periodic Table of Toasts published by JFA, a Lexington, Virginia-based marketing communications company, http://www.jfamarketing.com. The poster, part of a series based on the theory of Guerilla Linguistics created by John Freivalds, features toasts of 35 countries—from "Kippis" in Finland to "Gan Bei" in China—along with the label of each nation's representative drink, Finlandia Vodka and Tsingtao beer.

(January 2004)

"Reprinted with permission. All rights reserved. © Reuters 2004."

4

Humor Is No Laughing Matter

Pssst! Did you hear the one about the American businessman whose tame joke drew a hilarious response from his Japanese audience?

The American, curious why they liked the joke so much, later asked his official translator, who replied: "The joke was not appropriate, so I did not translate it. I simply said: 'The gentleman has told a joke. Please laugh.'"

It is not uncommon for interpreters to avoid translating humor.

"You have to be careful about jokes. They do not translate from culture to culture," said Sheida Hodge, worldwide managing director of the Cross-Cultural Division for Berlitz International Inc. in Princeton, New Jersey.

The American trademark is to start a speech with a joke, she said. "When foreigners speak here, they also want to start with a joke, but that never works because the worst thing you can do is mimic other people or the nuances of their culture."

The dos and don'ts of foreign cultures can get complicated for travelers, who need to beware of taboos dealing with gender, colloquialisms and body language.

"Humor is something we all need to make the world a better place, but it can also make life worse, if mishandled," said Steve Norcliffe, commercial director of the Queen Elizabeth II Conference Center in London.

"You may think you know a nation after spending a lot of time there, but you cannot be fully up to speed with the latest happenings, thoughts, etc," said Norcliffe. "And, sure as heck, you'll choose a no-go subject matter for a humorous quip just when you are near to closing the deal."

In some cultures, humor can be seen as aggression or dominance, so it would be a faux pas for a woman to tell a joke, said Patti Wood, an international speaker and trainer also known as the Body Language Lady (www.pattiwood.net).

A smile, often the best ice breaker, is not necessarily a sign of approval, said Wood. "For Chinese, Japanese and Malaysians, a 'masking smile,' with corners of the mouth turned down, is a polite way of letting you know what you are doing is not appropriate."

The eyes also play a role in cross-cultural communication.

Ed Ruggero, an author and keynote speaker on ethical leadership, admits to having anxious moments while addressing the Choctaw Nation at a casino complex in Mississippi.

"Whenever I tried to make eye contact with someone, he or she looked down. It was very unsettling," he said. Later, a woman explained that Choctaw do not look strangers in the eye.

In some Asian cultures, an entire audience might close their eyes, said Berlitz's Hodge. "But it only means they are concentrating on what is being said and is a sign of respect."

It's important to make an effort to understand other cultures, but trying too hard to fit in with the locals can result in embarrassment on both sides.

During his work stint in the United States, Englishman Norcliffe, eager to show he knew the local lingo, glibly suggested a sales prospect could "brown bag" a brochure. "I thought it meant throw it in the trashcan. I didn't find out until after the meeting that I was way off the mark."

Wood agrees that humor varies from country to country.

"Americans, because we are individualistic and confident, tend to do a lot of put-down humor," she said.

"It's also a big deal for the British; they believe it breaks tension," said Hodge. "But their sense of comedy is different. They use more irony, which Americans may mistake for sarcasm."

Ethnic or gender-related humor is still acceptable in some parts of the world, but in U.S. business meetings and presentations, you've got to keep it clean.

"That means no off-color jokes," said Hodge. "Sometimes Europeans make sexual innuendo jokes, but that doesn't go over well with Americans. And ethnic jokes are out."

The solution is simple, says Ruggero: "Don't use jokes. Use humor. A joke requires a response. If I make a humorous comment, at least some of the people will laugh."

If a joke bombs, body language speaks louder than words.

"Basic arm folding is seen as putting a barrier between you and the person who is talking," Wood said.

There are still times, however, that no matter how hard you try to do the right thing, it gets lost in translation.

Ruggero tells the story of a newly promoted American soldier at an embassy party in France celebrating the Allied victory at the end of World War II.

"A Frenchman stood up to give a toast and a British officer followed suit. Then a young major, who had studied French at West Point, was pushed front-and-center to represent the U.S.

"Unable to think of a toast, he chose a poem intended as a tribute to a child and his mother. 'The best years of my life,' he recited, 'Were spent in the arms of another man's wife.'

"His vocabulary was a bit rusty, however, and he confused the French words for arms and legs. Needless to say, the hosts were offended and the mortified young officer was spirited away to his troopship ... just before the dueling pistols came out."

In a social setting, it makes for a very amusing story. But in the context of global business, that kind of gaffe can be fatal.

(April 2004)

"Reprinted with permission. All rights reserved. © Reuters 2004."

5

The Well-Dressed Traveler

The aphorism "dress for success" has in recent years been worn down to a cliche. Or maybe it's just that its meaning, like fashion, has changed to keep up with the times.

"Nobody dresses anymore," Joseph Nunziata, U.S. sales director for Worth Global Style Network (WGSN) said. "Things have changed dramatically, even in the last year. Now everybody dresses down, financial clients as well. It's almost like, 'Why are you wearing a suit and tie?' It's full dress-down, and it doesn't look like it's going away for now."

"People are not as locked in as years ago," said Nunziata, who should know. His company, a multilingual online business-to-business fashion news and trend information service (www.wgsn.com) has been described as "the fashion industry's secret weapon."

And other companies are recognizing its power. U.S. corporate subscribers are signing up at the rate of around 40 a month, and the list includes names such as Calvin Klein, Gap, Donna Karan, General Motors, DuPont and Hallmark.

But even with full dress-down the norm every day in some Wall Street firms, no one should think it means being unfashionable.

"Wearing a suit is easy," said Nunziata. "Dressing down is more difficult."

Dressed down is what Tim Zagat, co-founder and co-chair of Zagat Survey, likes to be while on the road. Whenever he travels on a plane, which is "at least 30 times a year," he wears khakis and a windbreaker and looks more like he's "going to a baseball game."

"If possible, I do not carry a bag that I can't fit into the overhead bin," said Zagat, whose guides provide consumer survey-based dining, lodging, nightlife and leisure information (http://www.zagat.com).

"I try to take as little as possible. And if I know I'm going to be on the road for any length of time, rather than having stuff cleaned in hotels at great expense, I'll have my clothes sent to where I know I'll be four or five days ahead."

Marilyn Carlson Nelson, the chairwoman and chief executive of Carlson Cos., always travels in style.

"For successful business persons, women and men both, it's always essential to make an immediate, positive first impression, especially when traveling internationally, where language and culture can present enough of a barrier in themselves," she said. "Tailored suits for business and elegant evening wear for functions are never out of place, no matter what the country."

As head of a company with operations in more than 140 countries, Carlson Nelson needs to budget her time carefully.

"My schedule is usually very organized, so I choose my wardrobe according to the functions I'll be attending. But, it's also important to be prepared for anything, so I pack liberally," she said. "I tend to favor fabrics that don't wrinkle, like wools, and those that don't show dirt—black or other dark colors. And I always leave clothes in the light plastic dry cleaning and laundry bags when packing. It eliminates wrinkles."

Carlson's businesses include Regent, Radisson and Country Inns & Suites hotels, Radisson Seven Seas Cruises, TGI Friday's restaurants, Carlson Wagonlit Travel, and Carlson Marketing Group.

Whatever the latest fashion trend or personal taste, frequent travelers must be flexible.

Douglas McKenzie, vice president of luxury sales for Starwood Hotels, "wouldn't consider" traveling to a business meeting without a "proper suit and tie." And the Scot never leaves home without packing cufflinks, collar bones and a special tie case to keep his ties in pristine condition.

Stephen Norcliffe, commercial director of Queen Elizabeth II Conference Centre in London, takes "a spare T or sweatshirt to change into, or a business shirt if I have to travel in a suit. And, in my flight bag there will also be a face cloth and water-based facial spray for rehydration."

The packing philosophy of John Rouse, editor and general manager of Capital-Gazette Newspapers in Maryland, is as uncomplicated as it gets.

"I pack only what I can fit into a carry-on bag, and it's always drip-dry, wash-in-the-bathtub clothes," he said. "In the summer, I travel in shorts ... I'm not going to waste a piece of business attire by wearing it on an airplane."

(July 2001)

"Reprinted with permission. All rights reserved. © Reuters 2001."

6

When Good Travelers Go Bad

In the air and on the road, tempers and epithets are flying almost as frequently as corporate travelers. It's a sign of the times.

High-powered executives hired for their smarts and paid to be globally resourceful are responding to a loss of dignity brought about by corporate cuts, heightened security measures and dwindling perks. On top of the daily grind of meetings and deadlines, it can add up to a bad attitude.

Research shows that 65 percent of passengers are finding rudeness a serious problem in travel these days. A study by Public Agenda, a nonpartisan opinion organization, also reveals that bad behavior is a major source of aggravation for transportation workers, 49 percent of whom have seen it threaten to escalate into a physical confrontation.

"Business travelers are more abrupt, more demanding—edgier and angrier," said Dr. Alan Hilfer. "They have a lower threshold from being poked and prodded and subjected to intense scrutiny. They are reacting to the pressure."

"Previously, there was a sense of entitlement," said Hilfer, the director of psychology at Maimonides Medical Center in Brooklyn, New York. "But cutbacks in amenities and even meals have brought resentment."

In the past, travelers thought they could get results if they made a big enough fuss. But today, that sort of behavior has the exact opposite effect on airlines, where hot-under-the-collar passengers may now be threatened with police action.

To head off problems, Virgin Atlantic Airways requires its frontline employees to take a Service Excellence course. Staff are trained to address customer issues using the H.U.G. I.T. approach: H-ear what the customer is saying. U-nderstand the problem. G-o with the flow by acknowledging the problem. I-nfluence with a positive energy. And, T-hank the customer.

Many people can find it stressful being confined with a lot of strangers on an aircraft. Trains, on the other hand, allow more freedom of movement and a better work environment, said Tim Roebuck, managing director of BritRail and vice president of sales for Norwegian Rail and Swedish Rail.

"Train travel is way less stressful. Boarding is quick, with two doors in every coach and a place to drop your bag inside. You can eat what you want, when you want it," he said.

"But anywhere, the more delays and the more congestion, the greater the propensity for people to lose their temper," Roebuck said, recalling a Florida flight where extended mechanical problems caused one frustrated passenger to jump up and down and demand to be let off the plane.

An encounter with a surly fellow traveler led to a black eye for corporate coach Penny Leigh, vice president of New York-based Frederick Knapp Associates executive development.

"I was on a late plane to Denver to conduct an executive image seminar," recalled Leigh, who has worked with more than 30,000 executives in the United States and Canada. "The man next to me stuffed his luggage and coat in the overhead bin, then put a huge briefcase on top of my clothes bag. I asked politely if he could put it somewhere else, but he grumbled 'No' and went to sleep."

When Leigh opened the bin before deplaning, the heavy briefcase slid out and hit her squarely in the eye, she said. "The man did not apologize."

The next morning, when she arrived to open the seminar for clients she was meeting for the first time, she was sporting a shiner as black as her business suit. Leigh, co-designer of American Management Association's course "Projecting a Positive Executive Image," was up for the challenge. Her opening words: "First impressions ... Are they accurate, or is it more important to be color-coordinated?"

Known for showing similar grace under pressure is a top concierge at London's Athenaeum hotel. In his 30-year career, Donald has seen and heard it all, yet he refrains from ever using the word rude to describe any guest behavior.

"What I see is more stress. With cell phones and e-mail, people don't have a second to escape," he said. "The other day, I heard an American lady tell her assistant 'We will not be available for 12-1/2 minutes today.' That really sums it up—everyone has a deadline.

"But, I truly do not let it get to me," Donald said.

When it comes to stress management, American travelers may have a more difficult time, says psychologist Hilfer.

"They tend to view things not as a privilege but as something they've grown to expect. Consequently they don't manage delays or slip-ups very well and take out their frustration on people that get in their way."

(March 2004)

"Reprinted with permission. All rights reserved. © Reuters 2004."

7

Deals on Wheels

A car, like a suit, makes a statement in the corporate world. Whether a business traveler sits behind the wheel of a luxury brand, an SUV, or a compact model, sends a powerful signal to clients.

The car—BMW, Jeep or Kia Rio—can be seen as an indicator of its driver's mood, personal or professional status and even sexual prowess.

"In the same vein that clothes make the man, whether true or not, a car means certain things," said Manhattan psychotherapist Lauren Howard. "To a client, it may say a lot about its driver, what kind of expense account they have, or how high up they are in a company."

The model, color or condition may even affect the course of negotiating a deal.

"When people see that someone is successful, there is an automatic bias that they must be good at what they do," she said.

As customers, business travelers are always in high demand. They are courted by hotels, airlines and car rental companies with offers of free parking, extra mileage points, tickets to sporting events and upgrades to a bigger, more powerful car.

In England, Virgin Atlantic's Upper Class passengers will have a chance to use amphibious limousines to go to London's busy Heathrow Airport (www.virgin.com).

The Royal Garden Hotel, next to Kensington Palace, has a silver/gray Daimler/Jaguar limousine for VIP clients' use. The general manager, Graham Bamford, drives his own BMW 5 series. When he travels abroad, however, practicality has the final word.

"I take business trips each year to the West Coast, from San Francisco to San Diego, and it is always my baggage which dictates the type of vehicle I have. And, a GPS navigation system is now a must, which immediately puts Lexus on the list of potentials," he said.

In his job, Bamford has noticed many guests using taxis and buses instead of hiring chauffeur or self-drive vehicles, suggesting that companies might be "trimming expense accounts."

"In the main, corporate accounts mandate that their travelers utilize intermediate size cars—a Chevy Malibu or Oldsmobile Alero—if traveling alone or with one colleague," said Susan McGowan, spokesperson for Cendant Car rental group, the parent of Avis and Budget, in Parsippany, New Jersey.

But, says Hertz spokeswoman Paula Stifter, "we also see companies consolidate rental needs into a car-pool situation, where three or four renters attending the same event share a larger vehicle like a full-size, 4-door, premium car or SUV."

"Executives may even rent a compact or mid-size car to arrive at internal meetings to drive home the cost-savings point to front-line employees," Stifter said.

Mike Wicks, commercial lines manager at General Casualty Insurance in Lincoln, Nebraska, drives the company car, a Chevy Malibu.

"It's plenty comfortable, but not overly expensive. It says that the company wants employees to have a good work environment, but is also expense conscious," said Wicks, who takes about 10 Midwest trips a year, plus one-day trips within Nebraska.

"Most corporate executives are keenly aware of the impression they present when seen driving a certain type of vehicle," McGowan said. "They want a vehicle that accurately depicts their own company image."

C. Edson Armi, an art historian and the author of "American Car Design Now: Inside the Studios of Today's Top Car Designers" teaches a seminar on contemporary American car design at the University of California at Santa Barbara.

Armi owns three cars—a 20-year-old BMW, a Volvo V70 2002 and a Mazda 6. His favorite depends on whatever his mood is on any particular day.

"Volvo is designed to calm you. The BMW is like a shot of testosterone; it makes you aggressive. Mazda is a nimble car that has the precision and delicacy one often associates with Japanese culture," he explains.

When traveling, Armi rents different kinds of cars—from the cheapest to the most expensive. "In Europe, I prefer a smaller car because streets are narrow and winding, so it should be nimble and maneuverable."

A Men's Car magazine survey of 2,253 Germans, ages 20 to 50, revealed that BMW drivers have more sex than owners of any other cars. Porsche owners have sex less often but are also the most likely to be unfaithful, the survey said.

Most of the time, when people rent a car for business, it really is only a means for transportation.

A person who normally drives a black Cadillac Escalade luxury SUV but rents a red Mustang convertible for a business trip might be trying to create an image, but not necessarily, psychotherapist Howard said.

"It depends on whether the car will be seen by clients. If not, it is a way of making that trip a bit more enticing as drivers experiment with a different way of looking at themselves. It doesn't mean they are unhappy with who they are ... it's just an opportunity to experiment."

(June 2004)

"Reprinted with permission. All rights reserved. © Reuters 2004."

8

Breaking the Language Barrier Overseas

Words: an arsenal of them, or just a few choice ones. Their power has never been greater than in today's global economy, where poor communication or neglect of cultural differences can result in a catastrophe of corporate proportions.

With distance being digitally eliminated, language remains among the last barriers to efficient global commerce. But how essential is it, really, for an American to speak a foreign language when doing business overseas?

"It isn't really, but it absolutely helps because it exceeds expectations," Anita Komlos, national director of business development at Berlitz International, says.

A former Berlitz student herself, she speaks four languages and is learning a fifth. Her English is so flawless that even Professor Henry Higgins would fail to detect her Danish origins.

"What's important is that people at least learn the basics, like greetings and introductions, in the local language. Since many would never expect an American to do that, it would get respect and admiration," Komlos said.

In business for 120 years, Berlitz has more than 450 locations in 60 countries. Some of its more illustrious students have included politicians such as the late Nelson Rockefeller and John F. Kennedy, business tycoon Lee Iacocca, entertainers Cher, Chubby Checker and Robin Williams, and writer Pearl Buck.

Corporate clients cut across every sector and include AT&T International, IBM, Boeing, Goldman Sachs, Johnson & Johnson, Mastercard, McDonald's and Philip Morris International.

The course most in demand all over the world, Komlos said, is English as a second language.

More practical advice on cross-cultural communication comes from Roger Axtell, public speaker and author of bestseller "Do's and Taboos Around the World" (John Wiley & Sons, Inc.), eight volumes covering useful topics such as

International Trade, Women in Business, Using English, Humor, Hosting International Visitors and Body Language, among others.

"Be very, very cautious. Particularly in the local vernacular, where the same words can mean different things in different countries," Axtell warns.

"The biggest problem is that Americans speak too fast. You can always tell a veteran international business executive by how slowly he speaks. Problems arise because English—the world's communication standard—is loaded with idioms, slang, jargon, buzzwords, acronyms and military and sports terminology. It is important to recognize that, for the listener, it is their second language and they can be easily overwhelmed."

Axtell recommends that Anglophones try to learn a foreign language. "At the very least, you will learn what the other person is going through."

Pronunciation is also critical. Imagine the stunned reaction at a U.S. lawyers' convention when the guest speaker—the president of a small foreign nation—expressed his immense pleasure at having the opportunity to address their "distinguished assembly of liars."

To prevent such gaffes and bridge the language divide that can hinder daily communication between foreign offices, language instruction sites are available on the Internet.

- The Enterprise Translation Server 4.0, available at http://www.TransparentLanguage.com from Transparent Language Inc., enables real-time cross-language communication and commerce in 23 languages. For instance:

"Japanese speakers can see an English-language document on the company intranet in Japanese. An English speaker is able to view a Russian-language e-mail in English. And an English speaker is able to receive an instant message in Spanish from a colleague, read it in English, and then send an English reply that his Spanish colleague can ultimately read in Spanish," CEO Michael Quinlan said.

- Berlitz's all-audio "Rush Hour" series of musical language courses is designed for listening "while driving, sitting on an airplane, taking a shower or even gardening."

"The music, rhythms and entertaining story lines will have listeners tapping their toes and speaking a language from the first lesson," said Ellen Adler, vice president of Berlitz Publishing, a division of Berlitz Language Services (http://www.berlitz.com).

(December 2002)

"Reprinted with permission. All rights reserved. © Reuters 2002."

Part II
RELATIONSHIPS

9

Absence Makes a Spouse Grow Sadder

The same trip that spells corporate success for the business traveler, frequently takes a personal toll on the spouse who is left home alone to cope with feelings of depression, loneliness or inadequacy.

"There are feelings of abandonment," says San Francisco-based therapist Daniel Ellenberg. The rational mind accepts the reasons the spouse must go away, but "there's another part of the brain that's a tunnel into the unconscious."

Childhood feelings of being left by Mom or Dad might be triggered, causing us to react defensively and even pick a fight with the spouse preparing to go out of town.

"The way we react often has nothing to do with the actual separation, but may, in fact, mask the real issues. It has to do with our core beliefs about ourselves—how important, competent or lovable we believe we are."

In his own marriage, Ellenberg, who is also the co-author of the book "Lovers for Life" is the one more often left at home. His wife, Judith Bell, a lead trainer for Will Shutz Associates, "is away at least one week a month," he said.

"The difficult part is re-entry," he says. "When you're alone, you get used to a certain rhythm."

After the homecoming, couples need to set aside time and space for each other to adjust mentally and emotionally.

"The most difficult time for me was usually the first few days after he came home," said graphics designer Carol Caputo, who met her husband, John Lawton, in Hong Kong 23 years ago. As president of Wearfirst Sportswear Inc., he makes about six trips a year to Asia for one to two weeks at a time.

"I was so anxious to tell him everything that had happened and wanted his emotional support. It was hard to leave him alone for a few days until he had time to recover," said Caputo, who made the choice to stop traveling when they decided to have a family. "I wasn't going to change his career because I had changed my own. If you love someone, you don't do that."

She has her own Manhattan-based visual communications firm that creates, designs and launches Internet Web sites and print and television commercials.

"We are very close, but we each have our own interests," says Caputo, concluding that, for her, "absence definitely makes the heart grow fonder."

"We've been on a 23-year date, and my husband is the greatest date in the world. You can't change a guy who's been traveling all his life. Now I'm more worried about what I'll do when he retires."

For some other couples, however, being separated over a long period of time doesn't necessarily make it easier.

For the better part of their 24-year marriage, Joyce and Joe Salemi have spent the work-week apart. The considerations were careers, home and eventually children.

"We've always had daily contact, but it's an unorthodox way of living. I wouldn't recommend it," Joyce said, adding that she has sought professional help to deal with her feelings.

Since September 11, she has "become more anxious" about Joe, an account representative for a major New York graphic arts company. "It's not on my mind daily, but frankly I'd like to see him here in Rhode Island," Joyce says.

Dawn Ortell, an investment banker in New York has traveled extensively on business for about 10 years.

"I travel at least a third of the time, generally domestically, but occasionally to London or Germany," she said.

Her husband of 15 years works in the oil industry as a sales executive.

"Victor misses me," she says. "But we have no children and no additional logistical issues. We are also unusual in that we live apart during the week. It's a dual career thing. We split our time between our apartment in Manhattan and home in New Jersey, where he works, and see one another on weekends."

"We were both independent when we got married and accustomed to traveling in our jobs. We work very hard and are willing to do what it takes to get ahead in our careers, and yet we pay attention to our relationship. We talk every night no matter where we are in the world and make sure we have quality time for one another on the weekend. We also take quiet time vacations alone together at least once a year. We go hiking where there are no cell phones," Ortell said.

Ray Jacobi, Chief Operating Officer of Dallas-based Rosewood hotels, manages properties on five continents worldwide. He and Ashley Cop have been together less than two years. To head off any separation-related problems exacerbated by his work, which requires him to travel "80 percent of the time," she quit her job as a contract employee for an advertising agency and now travels with him. Their last two-week trip took them to London, Zurich, St. Moritz, Berlin and Saudi Arabia.

But not all couples are so lucky.

Divorce lawyer Gerald Goldfeder, of Goldfeder and Abraham LLP in Bayside, New York, says: "In 35 years of practice, I've found that when people are apart, they tend to find companionship elsewhere."

"It's difficult to say which one is more likely to stray, but the real distinction I've seen has to do with age. The younger the couple, the more the separation tends to make the heart anxious for the return of the spouse. As couples get older, say in their 40s or 50s, they tend to find others who are 'traveling' in their own circles," Goldfeder said.

A study of medical insurance claims submitted by the spouses of World Bank employees over a period of 12 months revealed the level of stress-related and psychological problems was three times higher for those whose partners travel.

There is no one-size-fits-all solution, says psychologist Ellenberg. "That's when awareness of core issues becomes a crucial step. Some people can make things better by inner coaching, telling themselves 'I am significant' or finding ways to feel so. People who suffer physical discomfort may employ self-soothing reaffirmation while placing their or partner's hand on the affected area—the stomach, chest or head."

The traveling spouse can help by asking their partner what he or she can do to help them feel more significant or lovable, Ellenberg said. "But, it's very important to ask. Don't assume."

While frequent trips may seem glamorous to many, traveling on business is a trade-off. Various surveys have also found that globe-trotting executives:

- Feel guilty about abandoning their families.
- Have refused to go on a trip if it conflicts with their children's birthdays or school functions.
- Work longer hours—sometimes nearly double—while on the road.
- Don't like traveling with the boss.
- And, one-third would stop going on business trips "tomorrow" if they were assured it wouldn't hurt their career.

(April 2002)

"Reprinted with permission. All rights reserved. © Reuters 2002."

10

Emotional Tradeoff for Traveling Moms

An out-of-town trip may be one of the rare times a working mother can take a leisurely bath without barricading the door. Spa treatments, museum crawls and five-star restaurant dinners satisfy guilty pleasures she can't enjoy at home, while new places and new faces stimulate her mind.

Yet, underlying it all is a tough emotional decision every traveling mom faces: Will choosing a sweet business deal over sticky kisses damage her relationship with her children, as some studies show.

An American Psychological Association study published in the journal Developmental Psychology has found, however, that "a mother's level of education is a strong predictor" for her "being sensitively attuned" to her children.

Indeed, many professional moms say their children are actually more well-rounded individuals and less prone to separation anxiety because they keep them involved in their travel plans.

"If mothers have started a protocol of going to work every day, research seems to show there is no effect," said Dr. Jeffrey Fagen, a psychology professor at St. John's University in New York.

As Tara Innes juggles her work responsibilities, making sure her 8-year-old son, Will, doesn't feel left out is a priority for the managing director at Fitch Ratings in New York, who spends 20 percent of her time traveling to major U.S. cities.

"I have always traveled, and I think Will is accustomed to it," Innes said. "He probably learned the major cities in America before other children his age. He also learned dates and the days of the week by reading a map and detailed itineraries, she added.

"On the road, I get a lot of work done, and I love getting a good night's sleep, something I don't always get at home," said Innes, whose job routinely takes her to Los Angeles, Denver, Dallas, Boston, Chicago and Washington. "But overwhelmingly, I miss my family."

For Julie Wagner of Johnstown, Pennsylvania, a captain in the U.S. Army Reserve and mother of two, duty comes first.

"My children were born into the Army and are used to my traveling," said Wagner, who is planning to go to South Korea for 17 days of training.

All along, she has helped Zachary and Allison, now 17 and 15, deal with the separations by putting up a map and talking with them about her next destination. She also never misses the opportunity to bring back souvenirs—T-shirts for Allison and coins for Zachary to add to his collection.

Wagner's day-to-day job, as a non-uniformed school resource officer for the Johnstown Police Department, also requires her to travel, but the trips are often nearby and shorter.

"If it's military, it could be for two to three weeks. With the police job, two days to a week," said Wagner who travels four or five times a year, mostly for training and conferences.

"When the kids were small, it wasn't so bad," she said. "Now that they're older, I miss them more because of their activities. Even if I'm exhausted, I call home to see how the saxophone or guitar lessons went. Allison is a great goalie on her soccer team."

"Wherever I am, I relax by going shopping—mostly for them. It's fun to look for something special for the kids and for my husband. And, for once, the bathroom is all mine!"

Long-term deployment of up to a year looms as a possibility, but Wagner takes it in stride.

"We'll deal with it," she said. "It's my job."

Julie Zegras, a retail buyer and merchandiser, never takes a day off from her toddler sons Trevor and Griffin. It's her choice.

"I miss them and don't feel comfortable going away without them," she said from one of her Connecticut shops. "Trevor has been traveling since he was 4 weeks old and will go anywhere. He's a pleasure to travel with, he's so well adjusted."

Zegras selects contemporary women's clothing for 10 stores, including seven privately owned specialty boutiques called Rags in New York, Massachusetts, Rhode Island and Connecticut.

"I visit our stores in the Hamptons, on Martha's Vineyard and Block Island seasonally, between May and September," she said. "I go twice a year to Los

Angeles for two of the biggest fashion trade shows and maybe once a year to Atlanta."

Zegras considers herself very lucky that her employer pays for a full-time nanny, who happens to be her mother, to travel with her.

"My husband and I went away for two days for a work-related trip to Vail (Colorado). We didn't ski, but I went to the spa for a Swedish massage, pedicure, manicure and herbal wrap," said Zegras, adding that she has been separated from her sons only twice, the longest for three days.

"The key," says Dr. Fagen, "is that the child be in the care of a warm, caring adult who knows how to behave in an age-appropriate way toward the child. If the child feels secure and loved, there should be absolutely no problem."

(February 2004)

"Reprinted with permission. All rights reserved. © Reuters 2004."

11

The Road Test for Fidelity

Stress, separation and too much time on their hands may lure business travelers to look for love in all the wrong places, and for the wrong reasons.

"Some men—and increasingly women—say they cheat because life on the road is lonely," says attorney Sy Reisman, whose New York firm has been practicing matrimonial and family law for more than 40 years.

Relationship therapist Dr. Bonnie Eaker Weil, who has written two books on the subject, says the problem is more common than you think.

"The most prevalent calls I get are 'My husband/wife is traveling and I think he/she is having an affair. The answer is usually 'yes,'" Weil said. "More than 50 percent of all married women and approximately 70 percent of married men cheat on their mates at some point."

Frequent business trips can exacerbate the problem.

"Brain chemicals are affected by stress, time zones, heat and separation from family. When lonely, travelers tend to drink more. Alcohol lowers inhibitions, and sets off a cascade of hormones," she said.

Her research also reveals that "62 percent of men are more amorous in hot climates. They sweat a lot and tend to eat a lot of sugar or comfort food loaded with carbohydrates." Look out, she says, for business trips to California.

People with a lot of time on their hands try to fill the empty space.

"Stress, loss and separation create a biochemical craving for connection," Weil said.

Others take the view that, depending on the circumstances, it may not be the normal course for a man to remain loyal to one mate.

High-profile New York divorce attorney Raoul Felder, who has an impressive roster of clients from the corridors of power, put it bluntly: "It's about power. As you get progressively richer or more famous, the rules no longer apply. The girls fight over you," he said. "Anyway, it's not like it's a disease or unattractive. It feels good."

Power comes with a certain arrogance, he added.

"The guy might run a billion-dollar company, but he's careless enough to come home with lipstick on his collar. It's an act of selfishness. It's almost like the ultimate act of power is to force a spouse to tolerate it," he said.

American culture is also seen as more puritanical than, say, European culture.

A European hotel executive brushed aside the fidelity question with: "When we book conference facilities, we don't ask what participants plan to do in their free time. It's none of our business."

In Singapore, a masseuse may be offered as a courtesy to visiting executives.

Over the years, the law firm, Reisman, Peirez & Reisman in Garden City, New York, has also found that many adulterous spouses insist their affair is merely physical and has no bearing on their commitment to the family.

"It's not necessarily that they are unhappy. They get caught up in the moment, maybe the atmosphere of a romantic foreign destination—sightseeing, music, culture, food," Weil explained. "But, it's usually a cry for help; there is an underlying emptiness."

Business people are more likely to have one-night stands. They use sex as "medication"—especially if they're jetlagged. "It's like a shot in the arm, or a chocolate high, to get them through the next meeting," she said.

Sometimes, hotel staffers find themselves in the middle.

A former Colorado hotel employee said it is not uncommon for "repeat offenders" to slip a bill to a front-desker to either give expedient access to a specified visitor, or put any incoming phone calls into automatic voicemail for a given period of time.

The electronic age may have made life in general a lot easier, but it can make infidelity more difficult. Cheaters are more likely to get caught because of charges they made on their credit cards, or calls placed on their cell phones, to phones with caller ID, or e-mails sent to/from their home computers.

Here are some warning signs from Weil, a.k.a. the "Adultery buster":

- Traveling a lot and not leaving an itinerary—no hotel phone number, only cell phone or beeper.

- Sending flowers and calling six or seven times a day is a BIG warning sign, she says. "Don't mistake guilt for generosity and love."

"Dr. Bonnie" also gave ways for travelers to "adultery-proof" a business trip.

- Carry a sexy photo of your spouse.

- If traveling with a co-worker of the opposite sex, don't drink, don't flirt and don't do short outings together or spend time alone in either of your rooms. In short, don't do things that could be tempting.

- Finally, picture the person across the table from you 100 pounds heavier and 10 years older. Then ask yourself: Do you really want to jeopardize the rest of your life for one moment of pleasure?

Weil is the author of "Adultery, the Forgivable Sin" and "Make Up, Don't Break Up."

(August 2002)

"Reprinted with permission. All rights reserved. © Reuters 2002."

12

Friends Behind Bars

By profession, they are Hong Kong lawyers, military analysts, United Nations diplomats, and surgeons, but in the mental dossiers of good bartenders these out-of-town customers are also parents, golfers, cancer patients and broken-hearted lovers.

Business travelers arriving in a new city often head for the nearest watering hole and make friends with the guy behind the bar. The relationships are mutually beneficial.

"I have customers who live in the Netherlands, San Francisco and Vancouver who I consider regulars," said Frank Stanley, at the Palm Too steakhouse in New York.

In his 24-year tenure, he has developed an astonishing memory for names, faces and drinks preferences.

"When patrons are recognized outside their own turf, they feel comfortable and are likely to return," said Stanley, who can spot out-of-towners the moment they walk in the door. "I listen to cadence of speech, accents, the topic of conversation. I can tell from manner of dress and body language if they're from Germany or Italy. It's a matter of keeping your eyes and ears open."

In Washington D.C., one reason patrons hurry to the Round Robin bar in the landmark Willard Intercontinental is the chance to light up a cigarette. Another is hotel barman Jim Hewes.

"They've been traveling for hours and with no smoking allowed in planes or restaurants, they're eager to light up and relax with a drink," Hewes said. "Corporate travelers have a mindset. They want to conduct business with as few distractions as possible and look for creature comforts that remind them of home, even when crossing cultural lines."

Consistency and service are important across the board, though tipping patterns can vary by individual customer or location.

At the Bonaventure Brewing Co. on the pool-deck level of the Westin Bonaventure, high above the Los Angeles financial district, Nate Morris mixes "killer cocktails" for corporate travelers, who make up half of his clientele.

The foreign ones are "notoriously bad tippers," he said. "But the American guy on the company tab is worlds different—a little more congenial and a lot more generous."

Palm Too's Stanley does not perceive a difference.

"A ton of people who live in London come to New York—it's almost a suburb in the financial services world," he said. "Some are always concerned with making sure the server is adequately compensated. Others have a standard double-the-tax rule. Frequent customers tend to be more generous."

Americans are the most generous tippers in the Whisky Bar at London's Athenaeum on the edge of Mayfair. Bartender Matias Brizuera listens attentively to the problems of his regulars—consultants and blue-chip company executives—while maintaining a respectful distance, as required by hotel policy.

Upholding his hotel's reputation for discretion is also important to Jim Hewes, who in 20 years at the Willard, just two blocks from the White House, has been "in position to hear and see things."

"We get D.C. lawyers, lobbyists, trade unionists and political operatives who in the course of business look for a comfortable environment where they don't have to worry about people listening in," he said.

It's about growing relationships, says Bruno Marini, food and beverage manager of the Federalist restaurant at XV Beacon Hotel on Boston's Beacon Hill, which attracts the city's power elite as well as guests from Switzerland, Great Britain, Australia, New Zealand and all parts of North America.

"You get to know their likes and dislikes. Our conversations run to a day at work, the family, our single-malt Scotch collection or the extensive beverage list." The Federalist is known for its 21,000-bottle wine cellar.

"Guests run the gamut—headhunters, real estate developers, successful dot-com retirees," Marini said. "Some stay a couple of times a month. Five or six clients are here 10 to 12 days every month. They know they'll be well taken care of."

It's a self-fulfilling prophecy, says Frank Stanley. "What's good for the customer is good for the server and beneficial for the house."

For any establishment, return customers play a significant role.

"True-blue regulars pop in whenever they're in town. Those folks make my job fun. They make me feel that I've made some kind of impact," said Morris, whose personal favorites include Greg from Chicago, a flirtatious Alabama lady and the women's clothing store owner from Washington.

Morris also sees it as an investment in his own future.

Many travelers are shocked to find that downtown L.A. has little or no nightlife, he says, so he points them to hipper, cooler destinations.

"I figure one day I'm going to be this guy on business in London or Tokyo. And I know I could sure use a well-informed bar guy or girl who can tell me the ins and outs of the city."

(August 2004)

"Reprinted with permission. All rights reserved. © Reuters 2004."

13

Traveling With, or Without, Your Best Friend

In the fashion business, designers and supermodels travel in style with their pet pugs and poodles. But if your name isn't Valentino or Eva Herzigova and your pet can't go with you on frequent trips, you may have a problem.

Consider these facts: 62 percent of U.S. households own pets—there are more Americans with pets than with children; The 2000 U.S. Census reported 82 million men and women in the United States are single, and that about 40 percent of the work force is unmarried.

Applying that formula, it stands to reason that a significant number of single business travelers have pets and routinely face the problem of finding someone to take care of them in their absence.

The solution is to do what business people are good at doing anyway—establish a network.

"Find other pet owners with similar needs," recommends Dr. Amy Attas of City Pets the House Call Vets, in New York.

Meredith Harper's job as vice president for private sales of Impressionist and 20th-Century art at Christie's auction house, requires her to travel "fairly extensively" within the United States and abroad to places such as England and Switzerland.

It means that for three to five days every month, she has to leave her beloved Shepherd mix, Bella, at home.

"She has never stayed in a kennel," said Harper, who adopted Bella from a shelter at the age of 10 weeks.

Harper considers herself lucky. Her dilemma is shared by a neighbor, whose dog Colie, a chocolate labrador-husky mix, regularly swaps stayovers with Bella.

If both neighbors need to travel at the same time, Harper's mother or brother house-sit. In any circumstances, the dogs stay in the building and their daily routines, which include an afternoon pickup by the dog walker, remain largely undisturbed.

"Owners should customize care for individual pets," Dr. Attas advises. "If you have a young, active, healthy dog, the best thing is to get it involved in some kind of group daycare. Then, when you have to go out of town, it can stay there, and it's not much of a change from the regular environment."

"The local vet often has a technician or animal nurse who can come to the home and baby-sit for a fee," Attas said. "But, it is really important to leave your itinerary with whoever is caring for your pet. The traveler should be reachable or designate someone who can make any important decision regarding the pet's care."

Anitra Frazier, author of "The New Natural Cat" takes a novel approach—the pet's point of view.

"If you keep to a certain schedule and then you go away, the animal, from his perspective, may decide you have been attacked and killed by a predator. They don't know about flight delays or out-of-town conferences," she said.

But there are things you can do to calm them.

"I suggest leaving behind a piece of clothing you've worn—pajamas are perfect. For a cat, familiarity breeds contentment," said Frazier, whose popular book has been revised and expanded and includes holistic cat care, grooming tips and solutions to common as well as "impossible" problems.

"If you're going to be gone three weeks or a month, it might be better to board in a home-like situation, but hopefully never in a cage. Being caged is very stressful for a cat," she said.

Frazier also advises instructing the sitter to leave the radio on a classical station, and a different light bulb burning each day so the animal gets a feeling of change and movement, not a static environment.

"We realize that many single professionals travel with their pets and that vacationing guests can't bear to leave Fido home alone," said Michelle Payer, area director of public relations, The Ritz-Carlton Hotels and Resorts of Miami.

To meet that need, Miami's Ritz-Carlton, Coconut Grove, has developed a dog program.

"Guests can hire the Bow Wow Butler to exercise their pet at the nearby bayfront dog park, take it for a grooming with a Coconut Grove doggie spa basket (massage brush and aromatherapy shampoo) and then back to the room for poochie sushi and other cocktail-hour treats," Payer said.

On the "Bones 'N Bits" dog menu, one of the selections—steamed rice, broccoli and chicken—is called "Churchill's favorite," named for the general manager's dog, who taste-tested the items, which also include Oatmeal Kiss (crunchy oatmeal and peanut butter dog bone) and Jet Lag Cure (Iams lamb and rice-meal dry food.)

When it comes to pampering pets, no one does it better than the French.

"Dogs are very welcome as are any other pets—and free of charge, regardless of their size," said Claudia Schall, public relations manager of the historic five-star Hotel Meurice on the Rue de Rivoli on Paris' Right Bank.

"There is no special dog menu, but room service recommends "filet de steak" or "entrecote" of an equal quality to that served in the restaurant. Chef can also add seasonal vegetables or rice in order to make a balanced meal," she said. "As soon as the guest has made a reservation, our agent will find out the age of the pet and its preferred food."

Bellboys exercise dogs in the famous Tuileries Gardens opposite the hotel, which has hosted Franklin D. Roosevelt, Queen Victoria, and Salvador Dali and his pet ocelots.

In the South of France, the story is told of a frequent woman guest who accepted a glass of champagne on arrival, but refused a crystal dish of tap water for her dog.

"Mais, non," she sniffed, "My dog drinks only Evian."

On a more practical note, the AAA has helpful advice on air travel for pets, including questions for owners to ask:

- What is the airline's animal welfare policy?
- Is your pet fit to fly? Dogs and cats must be at least 8 weeks old. Very old, pregnant, ill or injured animals should not fly.
- Will the airline insure your pet?

AAA also recommends that travelers with pets reserve well in advance, if possible, tell the flight crew if your pet is in the hold so the pilot will activate the heater, and be considerate of seatmates by alerting them to your pet's presence in case they are allergic and want to change seats.

(August 2002)

"Reprinted with permission. All rights reserved. © Reuters 2002."

14

In the Corporate Trenches

Corporate warfare requires the leadership qualities of Patton, the military genius of Napoleon and the eloquence of Churchill. Yet ultimate victory cannot be achieved without teamwork.

The modern warriors that companies are hoping to draft ideally possess talent, knowledge, experience and commitment. To maximize those qualities in the office environment, CEOs look to outside team-building activities that emphasize competition, initiative, strategic planning and cooperation.

Fighter Pilots USA—the "ultimate corporate team builder"—caters specifically to corporations with customized programs of aerial combat that put executives at the controls of real fighter training planes using laser sights to achieve "kills". It's not a simulation and, "except for the bullets, everything is real."

"We fly to their program. Corporations tell us where they'll be and I tell them what we can do—in line with restrictions from the FAA," said Lee Abernethy, president and CEO of Chicago-based FPUSA.

Safety is the priority, and skilled F-16 pilot-instructors sit alongside to keep it that way.

"All our pilots are Certified Flight Instructors. Most of them are now commercial pilots on vacation; all have gone through check rides and are familiar with the equipment," he said.

FPUSA's fleet includes 6 T-6 Texans, one SF260 Marchetti, 4 Extra 300Ls and one P-51C Mustang.

"The minimum sortie count is eight and we can fly as many as 30-plus in one day. A package for an eight-sortie, full-day event, which can involve dinner and a reception, might be in the neighborhood of $8,000, though costs vary," said Abernethy, one of the original investors when the company was formed 11 years ago.

FPUSA, whose Web site is http://www.fighterpilotsusa.com, has drawn enthusiastic response from groups within companies such as Sprint, MSN Gaming Zone, American Isuzu Motors and General Motors' Fleet and Government Sales.

Warriors also learn useful dogfight lingo such as "Check your 6!" which, back on terra firma, means "Watch your back."

Laser-tag fever is sweeping across America, where there are now more than 500 laser-tag emporiums filled with booming sound effects and swarming with teams of light-phaser toting professionals from blue-chip companies such as Merrill Lynch, Chase Manhattan and Vanity Fair.

Inside the fog-shrouded mazes of the futuristic battleground, suited-up teammates must remain in constant communication, shouting encouragement or warnings to each other. And between games, they huddle in strategy sessions on how to best the opposition.

"It's a great team-building exercise because it forces you to work together in order to get the highest score possible for your team," said Claudia Geanas, event coordinator at New York's Lazer Park. "It's also a lot of fun. You get to shoot your fellow workers, or even your boss, and its legal!"

The 5,000-square-foot arena near Times Square can handle bookings for groups of 20 to 300. http://www.lazerpark.com.

Relationship-building is what drives the Minneapolis-based Carlson Marketing Group (http://www.carlsonmarketing.com), whose international capabilities span 22 countries. Targeting Fortune 1,000 companies, it not only identifies a client's business problems, it develops a strategic solution, executes a plan and measures the results.

"We focus on bringing people together to drive business results," Relationship Manager Margaret Murphy said.

One of their more remarkable examples was to help realize the vision of a U.S. financial services company's CEO "to build a global team in a global place."

"We arranged for a group of about 24 men and women executives and CEOs—hand-selected by the CEO from his customers—to go to Kenya. In the Maasai Mara region, they went to a village of about 300 and, working alongside villagers, helped to spruce it up. They did a lot of painting and rebuilding, fixing up walls and roofs and cleaning up debris. The effort to give back to the community was coordinated with several organizations over there.

"It was an opportunity to build relationships in a unique setting," Murphy said.

The project was so successful that participants have since returned with their families and kept up the relationships they established with the CEO as well as with local people, she said.

How does Carlson, one of the largest privately owned companies in the United States, handle team-building for its own employees?

"Last year, our senior execs and spouses (or a guest) were treated to an Alaska cruise on our then-newest ship, the Radisson Seven Seas Navigator," said Douglas Cody, corporate vice president public relations and communications for Carlson Companies.

"A few years earlier, the senior-most execs made a week-long sweep through the U.K. and Paris, again with spouses or a guest. One day, the schedule required the entire group to take a 7 a.m. train from London to Peterborough, tour an operation there, hop on a bus and fly to Paris in time for an evening function.

"On the bus ride to the airport, the group started whistling the theme from "Bridge Over the River Kwai" ... That's when I knew the team-building had truly taken place!" Cody said.

(July 2001)

"Reprinted with permission. All rights reserved. © Reuters 2001."

PART III
HEALTH

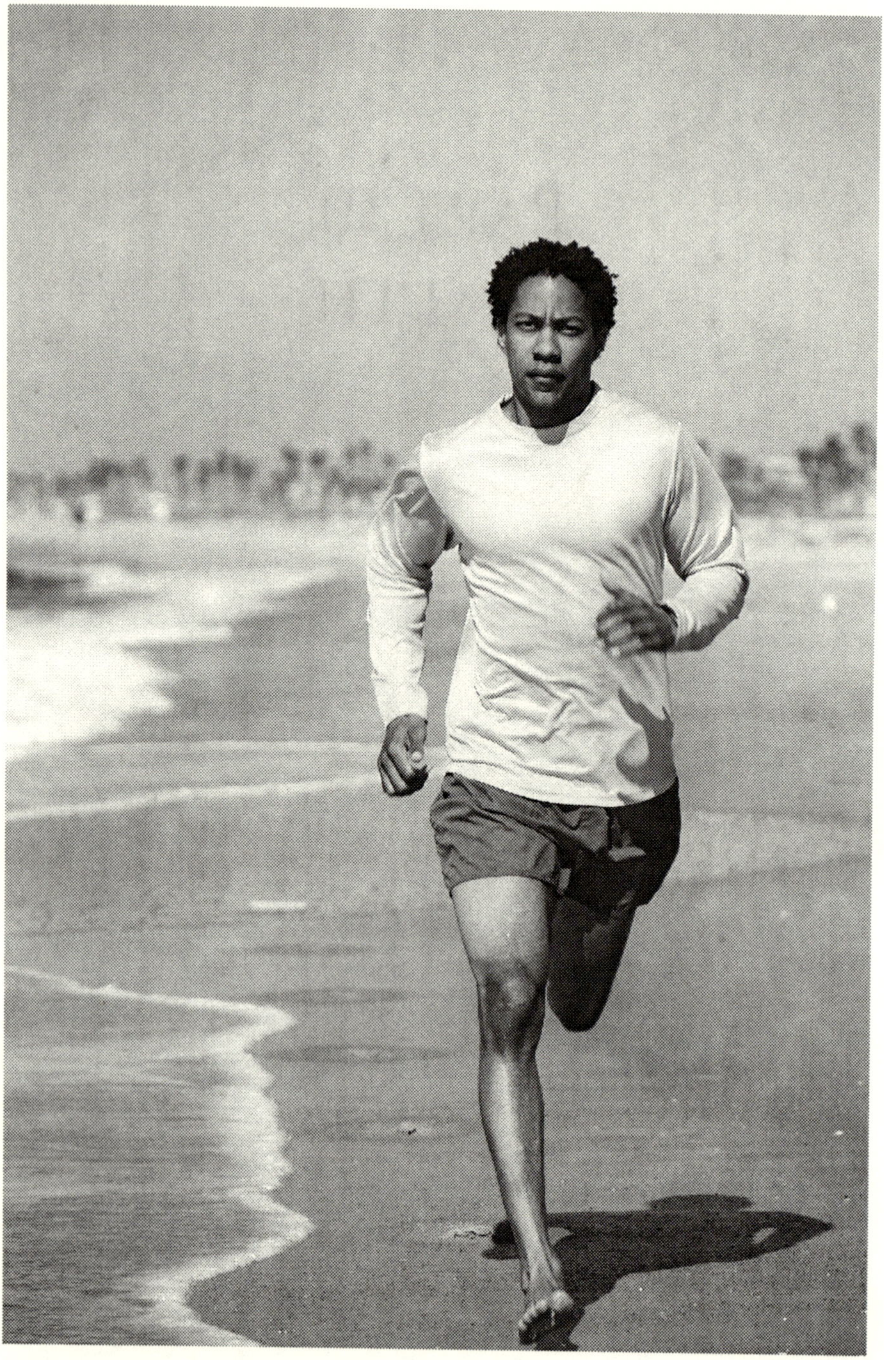

15

Don't Worry, Be Happy

All work and no play can make a business traveler dull and ineffective.

To be more productive and "keep the mental ax sharp," a leading psychologist says, do something that makes you happy.

"It's the No. 1 thing I recommend," said Dr. Carole Stovall, a Washington, D.C.-based psychologist whose client roster includes senior executives of Fortune 500 companies.

"Unless we take care of ourselves, the ax gets more dull and it takes more strokes to cut down a tree," she said. "So, we do ourselves a great service by keeping the ax sharp—by keeping ourselves happy and doing things that give us joy."

Accomplishing that can be as simple as packing your favorite classical CD, she said, or checking listings in the local newspapers for activities or things of interest that may be going on in the cities on your itinerary.

In keeping their nose to the grindstone, too many adults get trapped in the cycle of earn-and-spend, says medical scientist, psychologist and author Joan Borysenko. To help them break the cycle, her book "Inner Peace for Busy People" deals with ways to "stop Palm Pilots, cell phones, beepers, e-mails, and faxes from running your life."

"Variety is enormously important in life," said Dr. Frank Farley, recent president of the American Psychological Association. "A change can be as effective—and often more so—than a rest."

"People who don't relax can lose energy and creativity by staying so focused that they run out of juice," said Farley, an authority in the areas of motivation, human behavior and risk taking.

He suggests that breaking the pattern—say, by playing golf or attending a local sporting event—might get them out of the mental rut and send them back to work more refreshed.

Sports psychologist Dr. Patrick J. Cohn, president and founder of Peak Performance Sports of Orlando, Florida, said a common trait of business executives and athletes is that they are workaholics.

"Some athletes feel guilty if they skip training. It's the same in the business world, there's guilt associated with taking a day off," Cohn said.

While actual participation, such as playing a round of golf, is a better option than watching it on TV, there's an advantage to attending a sporting event ... it's more of a group phenomenon, he said. "It's about becoming immersed, escaping into that realm so that maybe for just a few minutes you forget about some of the demands or pressure of the workplace."

International business travelers in dogged pursuit of corporate deals may find them easier to achieve if they spend their leisure time soaking up a little local culture.

"An in-depth familiarity of a country's culture and customs almost always pays a direct benefit in terms of any executive's effectiveness in communicating successfully with a foreign counterpart," says Thomas Switzer, director of communications for the American Foreign Service Association in Washington, D.C.

Switzer, a retired senior foreign service officer and cultural attache in Europe and Latin America, also cautioned that a "negative perception of a foreign visitor is increased if that individual makes a substantial gaffe in interacting with a counterpart," making it all the more important to have "some degree of knowledge of meeting, greeting, speaking and dining habits" to avoid a needless misunderstanding.

Here are some recreational ideas for business travelers preparing to hit the road:

- In London, The British Antiques Dealers Association Fair is an annual springtime event in the Chelsea district. Tickets include one re-entry pass and a BADA Annual Handbook, a reference guide to dealers. (877-872-0778 or http://www.bada-antiques-fair.co.uk).

- In many major cities, Keith Prowse ticket company can arrange advance tickets for the theater, sightseeing, dining or special events such as the Chelsea Flower Show in London or the Edinburgh Tattoo in Scotland (800-669-8687, http://www.keithprowse.com) or http://www.visitbritain.com).

- China's Grand Hyatt Beijing has Feng Shui rooms, parking space for more than 10,000 bicycles, broadband TV, high-speed modem lines and movies on demand. In the heart of the business and shopping hub, the hotel is within walking distance of historic sites such as Tiananmen Square and the Forbidden City, once reserved only for the Emperor and his entourage. (http://www.hyatt.com).

- Furniture shopping can be fun in Denmark. The "father of Danish modern design" Arne Jacobsen items, from bowls to candlesticks to the classic Egg chair, are available in local shops. Or, arrange to have a home-cooked meal with a Danish family (about $45 at http://www.meetthedanes.dk). For other information, go to http://www.visitdenmark.com.

- The Iceland Naturally Food Festival kicks off a year of wholesome activities on the eco-island of waterfalls, mountains, geysers, hot springs and spas. (http://www.icelandnaturally.com, http://www.icelandculture.com or http://www.IcelandTouristBoard.com).

- Motor sports enthusiasts can catch a Formula One Grand Prix race in venues all over the globe: Australia, Bahrain, Brazil, China, Italy, the United States, Britain and Japan. (http://www.formula1.com)

- Ski-loving executives can enjoy Norway's national sport well into the spring. Some events: World Cup Alpine Skiing, Narvik Winter Festival, and Holmenkollen Ski Festival (http://www.visitnorway.com).

Finally, there is a hotel in Colorado's Rocky Mountains that caters to busy executives and vacationers alike by offering ski butlers to carry guests' equipment, help fit poles, impart information on the latest weather conditions and offer tips on where to find the best-groomed run or the most challenging moguls.

"We realize that guests—especially today—arrive here in varied states of stress. Our duty is to remove the albatross of the real world from their shoulders," says Richard McLennan, general manager at the St. Regis Aspen.

(January 2002)

"Reprinted with permission. All rights reserved. © Reuters 2002."

16

Making the Most of a Working Breakfast

Corporate travelers need to be alert and ready to deal from the moment they wake up. So, skipping breakfast is not recommended, nutritionists say.

"When you wake up in the morning, basically you have used up the energy sources from the day before, so you're starting with a low tank of gas," said Abby Bloch, a registered dietitian and nutrition consultant in New York. "To be efficient, your body needs to have a new supply of fuel."

Studies show that the morning meal replenishes blood glucose levels, improving concentration and problem solving skills so crucial to corporate road warriors, be they in Indianapolis or Italy.

At Le Meridien's Hotel Eden in Rome, General Manager Marcel Levy says breakfast is slowly replacing lunch as an "entertainment meeting" for reasons that make good business sense.

"Many of our business travelers take advantage of breakfast to meet with their colleagues in order to decide strategies for meetings later the same day," Levy said. "It's quicker, it doesn't cut the day in two, and it is more cost-effective."

Stressed-out travelers dealing with time changes, cultural differences or family concerns back home can't risk arriving for a foreign-office strategy session distracted and fatigued.

A power breakfast in some circles is also called "head-hunting hour," when bosses are known to screen candidates for senior management—particularly for posts dealing with offices overseas. What they're obviously looking for are decision makers who can think clearly right off the mark.

These sessions usually start at 7:30 or 8 a.m. and finish, not coincidentally, before the opening of local stock markets.

To prepare for an early meeting, business travelers can make life easier for themselves with a little preparation the night before, such as laying out the clothes they plan to wear—down to the socks and underwear. They can also arrange for a wake-up call 15 or so minutes earlier, allowing time to catch the top of a morning newscast while sipping a juice or coffee before showering.

If the strategy session is later in the day, some may prefer joining fellow travelers in the hotel dining room for the breakfast buffet.

"Today's travelers waste no time when taking breakfast. They are also looking for quality, health and vitality to start with," said Ezio Indiani, general manager in Geneva's Hotel des Bergues, where Le Pavillon restaurant and terrace overlook Lake Geneva and its famous water fountain.

"The aroma of fresh-baked croissants and coffee is just part of the hot and cold buffet: Scrambled eggs, Swiss cheeses, seasonal fruits, and of course, Bircher Muesli—a blend of berries, yogurt and cereals. A healthy corner has freshly squeezed juices. While not included in the rate, 60 percent of our clientele still choose to eat breakfast," he said.

"Breakfast is definitely important, but I'd recommend that people eat more protein and fat with a minimum of carbohydrate to avoid the sugar swing that would make them feel foggy a few hours later," Bloch said. "This is especially true for business travelers, who don't want to experience those peaks and valleys."

"Even a glass of skim milk and toast is predominantly carbohydrate so, a couple of hours later, they'll feel ravenous or irritable and have trouble concentrating," the nutritionist explained. "A better breakfast would consist of an omelet with lox or veggies and a half slice of dark grain or rye toast. Also, a small serving of melon or berries and coffee or tea."

For their first meal of the day, many Americans opt for the staples of cereal and milk, or bacon and eggs with toast. But seasoned travelers take the opportunity to expand their horizons by trying local breakfasts around the world.

- In Japan, at the Radisson Miyako Hotel Tokyo, there are three restaurants with breakfast menus tailored for guests from all over the world, said General Manager John Banta. All three offer standard Western fare, but ShiSen, a Szechuan Chinese restaurant, includes Chinese Breakfast: Okayu (rice porridge), Funyu, a fermented tofu that is "beyond unique in flavor ... like the tofu version of blue cheese," pickled daikon (radish), dried shrimp, Mibuna (wild spinach), Zatzai Chinese pickles, Shibazuke (eggplant and cucumber salad), assorted dim sum, and shiu mai fried tofu in Szechuan sauce.

California Cafe, an East/West restaurant, serves a Japanese breakfast of steamed rice, miso soup, Japanese style eggs (tamago), grilled fish, Nori Natto (fermented soy beans), pickles and green tea.

Yamatoya Sangen, has a choice of two kinds of Japanese breakfast: asa-kayu, a rice porridge eaten with salt and dried powdered seaweed, boiled egg, broiled fish, boiled vegetables and Japanese pickles. Or, steamed rice, broiled salmon, tamago (Omelet), baked Nori, seaweed, pickles and miso soup.

- The British serve a hearty array of meats—sausage, kidney, chops and bacon—eggs, grilled tomato, mushrooms and smoked fish as well as baked goods with honey and marmalade.

- In Scandinavia and northern continental Europe, the morning meal includes eggs, cold cuts of meats and cheeses, yogurt, a variety of breads with butter and jams. Swedes pour a slightly sour milk called filmjolk over their cereal.

- Austrians have a light breakfast very early and later eat a substantial one called Gabelfruhstuck (fork breakfast) in a coffee house.

- In Spain and Portugal, a roll with butter and jam and a cup of very light coffee is usually sufficient, although Spaniards also indulge in a combo of (thick, hot) chocolate con churros (deep-fried, cinnamon sugar-coated tubular doughnuts).

- Most South Americans prefer a light Continental-style meal, like Brazil's cafe da manha, which consists of a cup of very light coffee, sweet rolls and fruit.

- In East and West Africa, breakfast often includes uji, a thin cornmeal gruel.

Back in New York, Abby Bloch cautions against the wisdom of some grab-and-go breakfasts that are seemingly benign.

"A single bagel is equivalent to six or seven slices of bread. Add jelly and a glass of juice, and two or three hours later you are going to crash," she said.

(August 2002)

"Reprinted with permission. All rights reserved. © Reuters 2002."

17

Staying in the Comfort Zone

It takes more than the latest in-room tech toys and warp-speed Internet access to make a successful business trip. Comfort also ranks high among the needs of weary travelers.

Increasingly sophisticated umbilical cords that reach back to home offices are now so commonplace in hotels catering to business travelers that they cancel each other out.

So, in a never-ending quest to fill rooms, hotels continue to be on the lookout for ways to attract clients by combining the mandatory technology with harmonious surroundings.

Things are not always what they seem.

At a hotel in Italy, moving carpets encased in floors, virtual pictures playing on wall-screens, and large round bathtubs with televisions on their rims might appear to be beyond innovative, but they strictly follow the principles of Feng Shui (Wind/Water), the ancient Chinese art of achieving balance with the environment.

Gucci boutique designer Guido Ciompi, who created the extraordinary atmosphere at The Gray in Milan, adheres to the belief that if a building has good energy, its residents will be equally content. Guest suites have private workout rooms and a divan runs along the perimeter of the restaurant to ensure guests' comfort at mealtime.

The environmentally smart Sheraton Rittenhouse Square Hotel in Philadelphia claims to have something no other U.S. hotel has—clean air.

"The major complaint of frequent travelers is air quality," said environmental consultant and hotel co-owner Barry Dimson. "They go from bad air in an airplane to bad air in a hotel room. We have a large tank two stories above the hotel that pumps in filtered air every half hour—that's 48 times a day."

"Our bedding, drapes and sofa fabrics are made from organically grown cotton. The furniture has either water-base or baked oil-base finish; carpets are tacked down and wallpaper is put up with water-based glue," he said.

A frequent comment from guests is that "it's the best night's sleep we've ever had," Dimson added.

And, he noted, the hotel is energy efficient as well as profitable in a down market. "Environmental conferences seek us out because we practice what we preach. With fewer people traveling in general, attracting conference business is key."

Similar to Feng Shui, the connection between space, color and energy is at the core of Vaastu Shastra, a 5,000-year-old Hindu belief that has been employed in the construction of Hyatt hotels in India.

"A Vaastu master has been involved during the initial design of some of our Indian hotels, providing important input on the locations of the entrance, gardens and building elevations," said John Shamon, Hong Kong-based director of technical services for Hyatt International-Asia/Pacific.

"Our Indian owners are firm believers in the principles of Vaastu and made extensive modifications to the main entry of the Hyatt Regency Mumbai," Shamon said. "The entrance has a sharp 90-degree turn and will have a very small (1/8 inch) red light to conform to the principles of Vaastu."

Although practices such as Vaastu and Feng Shui apply primarily to building structures and interior spaces, there are elements relating to personal workspace and professional success that have also found enthusiastic response in the West.

In southern California, Tokyo-born Billy Yamaguchi, president and co-owner of Yamaguchi Enterprises Inc., has the distinction of being the first to apply Feng Shui principles in cutting and coloring the hair of his clients. With salons in spas and hotels, he caters to globe-trotting executives as well as professional athletes and movie stars.

"One of my clients was a woman from Microsoft," he said at Yamaguchi's in the Century Plaza hotel in Los Angeles. "We gave her a hairstyle and color that was in harmony with her personal energy, life style and environment."

Yamaguchi added that the highly personalized hair treatments have even helped his clients get jobs. "I know for a fact that in the last eight years they've always gotten the job they were going for."

Chicago-based Englishman John Wallis, senior vice president for marketing at Hyatt International Corp., says he is more comfortable at work and at home leading a "north-south" life, as determined by a formula using his birth date and Feng Shui.

"Having spent part of my life in Asia, I've wound up being a tiny bit spiritual and actually believe there is something to a lot of Chinese customs. Some may say it's superstitious, but I feel comfortable with it."

In Cologne, Germany, The Excelsior Hotel Ernst has a choice location—just opposite the city's magnificent cathedral. Its opulent interiors are mainly of historic origin and its service got worldwide recognition with the Five Star Diamond Award from The American Academy of Hospitality Science.

The hotel's success, says Managing Director Manfred Brennfleck, comes from a harmonious blend of traditional values with contemporary standards of comfort and service.

"We do not choose any colors or furniture under the principles of Feng Shui, but try to give our guests a feeling of a home away from home and, with that idea in mind, we choose colors that convey a certain warm and cozy surrounding. We figured out that the bright orange/yellow and golden tones have a kind of soothing effect on our guests," Brennfleck said.

(July 2002)

"Reprinted with permission. All rights reserved. © Reuters 2002."

18

Soaking Up Serenity

Water is hot. As pressured business travelers also find themselves frequently near the boiling point, savvy hoteliers know that water—in the form of a bath, a bottle, indoor pool or ocean view—is an ideal means for them to cool down.

Hence, water-based treatments promoting health, vitality and relaxation, flourish at luxury properties ideally situated near a river, lake or at the oceanside.

"Since the majority of the body is made up of water, it is a natural element for us," said psychologist Jeffrey Gardere, who has a radio show in New York. "It's natural for humans to enjoy something that we actually evolved from—as in the womb.

"The body and mind remember; muscle has memory, too. Water is calming and allows us solitude and quiet we don't normally get—like, say, in the shower or hot tub," the host of WWRL's "Conversations with Dr. Jeff," says. "It's why really stressed-out people take 20-minute showers. Warm water has the physiological effect of loosening muscles and calming nerves."

Using Miami's water environment as a classroom, Steve Geisz, director of recreation at The Doral Golf Resort and Spa, devised The Doral Regatta especially to develop trust, open communication and executive decision-making skills.

The Regatta is the culmination of a collaborative effort involving two teams from the same company—CEOs as well as administrative assistants—who are given materials to build boats, and then race them against each other.

"Corporations are our No. 1 clients, and this exercise fosters teamwork as well as the competitive spirit," said Geisz, whose clients come from New York and Pennsylvania as well as Latin America and Europe—places like Puerto Rico, Colombia, France, Italy and Germany. Notable participants have included General Electric, Falcon Jets, Pfizer and Glaxo-Smith-Kline, he said.

Another spa catering to corporate groups is Miraval Life in Balance, near Tucson, Arizona, where its state-of-the-art Catalina Conference Center can accommodate up to 120 people.

The resort's Mind Like Water mineral float bath removes external stimulation and soothes brain wave activity during 80 minutes of effortless floating to achieve a deep state of mental and physical relaxation. More than 100 jets are programmed to work on key areas of the body in the Hydrotherapy tub to detoxify, aid circulation and relieve muscle soreness.

Geographic location can provide a natural advantage.

- In Scandinavia, the Oresund Region, which includes greater Copenhagen in Denmark and Malmo in Sweden, is a magnet for high-tech and biotech conferences. The Oresund Fixed Link Bridge expediently connects the two cities by road and rail, making it possible for conference groups to cross the sound in just 25 minutes.

- In Italy, the canal system gives a competitive edge to Venice, where the Hotel Cipriani has a swimming pool with heated salt water. Portofino's Hotel Splendido overlooks the bay and harbor. Its new Health and Wellbeing Center and pool, surrounded by pine and olive trees, has panoramic views of the Mediterranean.

- London's waterways—90 miles of canals and rivers and 110 acres of docks—are a part of its broad-based appeal. The Dorchester hotel there serves herb-flavored water and, upon request, will provide a fridge full of a guest's favorite brand.

- The Orient-Express' Miraflores Park Hotel in Lima, Peru, has a Presidential Suite with dedicated bath butler service. Bathtime options begin with a half-hour massage while the butler draws the perfect bath using scented salts and oils. Scented candles are lit as pre-selected music plays in the background. Variations include bubbles, a glass of cognac, rose petals, champagne, and strawberries. When relaxation is complete, the butler stands ready with warmed towels, body lotions, and a bedside cup of hot chocolate.

- A menu with 21 kinds of water from all over the world is presented along with the wine list to diners in Le Park restaurant at Park Hyatt Paris-Vendome in France.

- Elevators rise from a golden mosaic-lined river in the lobby at the Park Hyatt Moscow, and Grand Hyatt Dubai features an indoor river, seven streams and a waterfall.

Water, particularly the ocean, mirrors the ebb and flow of how our hearts pump blood into our system, Gardere said.

"It is a cycle and part of the rhythm of life. When you focus on rhythm, it becomes an unconscious part of us and allows us an environment where it takes away stress."

(August 2003)

"Reprinted with permission. All rights reserved. © Reuters 2003."

19

When Work Is Done, a Play's the Thing

A night at the theater can be just the ticket for corporate travelers who have had their fill of high drama in busy airports and contentious boardrooms.

In a world of intense travel and big money deals, people need a coping mechanism, says Dr. Alan Hilfer, a psychologist at Maimonides Medical Center in Brooklyn, and going to the theater can be "extremely beneficial."

"These guys are frequently workaholics and overly involved with work. They need to give themselves time to laugh, to understand literature, have a conversation about something other than business," said Hilfer. "All work and no play makes them very uninteresting people."

Business travelers seeking balance from a demanding work schedule may find the solution in a hotel-theater package.

In Manhattan's Wall Street financial district, The Ritz-Carlton New York, Battery Park—where rooms have city or harbor views—arranges tickets and car service to Broadway shows.

The midtown Kimberly Hotel's Broadway Package I includes show tickets, a one-bedroom suite and continental breakfast. Add-ons available are limousine service to the theater and dinner in one of the city's top restaurants.

Amtrak riders arriving at New York's Penn Station can cross the street to the Hotel Pennsylvania, where the Penn 5000 Club is geared to business travelers' needs, with dedicated elevator service and a private executive lounge with high-speed Internet. The Broadway Package includes accommodations and tickets to a choice of hit shows.

In London, Show Time is the name of a winter getaway theater package at 51 Buckingham Gate Hotel, where corporate travelers make up 70 percent of the guests in the off-season.

"We decided to do a theater package because we are ideally situated and because of the success of two previous packages involving theater tickets," said manager Liam Ryan. "It is the ideal way to combine business with pleasure."

Show Time includes two nights in a deluxe junior suite, two top-price tickets to a show, pre-theater champagne and canapes, London black-cab transport to the theater and additional pampering in the form of butler service.

At the Park Hyatt Chicago, 85–90 percent of weekday bookings come from the corporate sector, said Jaro Fisher, director of sales. While most of the business is domestic, international clients come mainly from Canada and Japan.

Theater packages have been available since the hotel opened in June 2000, said Fisher, himself a theater buff who catches a show "a couple of times a month" and calls it "a most enjoyable escape." Included are two tickets to a performance at the new Lookingglass Theatre in Chicago's famous Water Tower, across the street from the hotel.

Prime location near business and entertainment venues in world capitals is a source of pride for Park Hyatt, according to executives at a gathering in New York.

The Park Hyatt Sydney, on the edge of Sydney Harbor has views of the Harbor Bridge and Opera House, an Australian landmark. "Our guests can arrive at the Opera by boat," said Ernesto A'de Lima, general manager.

The Ararat Park Hyatt Moscow is just minutes from the Kremlin, Red Square, the central business district and the Bolshoi Theatre—where the language of ballet needs no translation, and general manager Jiri Kobos promises that tickets for guests "can be provided on short notice."

A Musical Package at Le Meridien Vienna, near the Opera House and the Theater an der Wien, includes accommodation, breakfast buffet, dinner and tickets.

The choices are many and varied and pleading "not enough time" is not an acceptable excuse, psychologists say.

"Business travelers should take advantage of the opportunity to go to the theater. By relaxing, dining and socializing with other people they can cleanse themselves and recharge their batteries," says Hilfer.

(September 2003)

"Reprinted with permission. All rights reserved. © Reuters 2003."

20

Illness and Theft are Occupational Hazards

These days, when it comes to health or personal property, it is more important than ever for business travelers to keep in mind that it's better to be safe than sorry.

More than one-third of all international travel is work-related—much of it last minute, according to the U.S. Occupational Safety and Health Administration (OSHA). With a bit of common sense and by thinking like a thief, it may be easier than you think to avoid falling victim to illness or robbery while on the road.

"In the best of all possible worlds, a business traveler would anticipate the risks and take preventive measures," says Dr. Bradley Connor, a gastroenterologist and medical director for the New York Center for Medicine. "Even the most infectious diseases are preventable."

OSHA has issued a health bulletin on its Web site (http://www.osha.gov), warning business travelers of the risks of exposure to infectious diseases and recommending that they seek medical advice and take preventive measures.

"Many business travelers are neither adequately informed about the health risks they encounter nor receive proper medical guidance for prevention," OSHA cautions.

"The most important piece of advice: Always tell your doctor your travel history," said Connor, who is also executive board chairman of the Travel Industry and Public Education Committee. He has been a member of the International Society of Travel Medicine (http://www.istm.org) since its founding in 1991.

It makes sense for travelers to check with the company doctor or, even better, the Center for Disease Control (CDC) experts in Atlanta. Think of exotic bugs like yellow fever, dengue, and even tuberculosis. A shot in the arm might be painful, but it can save years of misery or even your life.

According to the World Health Organization, the most common vaccine-preventable diseases include hepatitis A and B, and the most significant infectious disease threat to global travelers is malaria, which is carried by mosquitoes.

Most at risk are visitors to areas such as Africa, Asia (except Japan), the Caribbean, South America, Central America, the Middle East, and eastern and southern Europe.

Health risks relevant to specific destinations can be found on the CDC Web site (http://www.cdc.gov/travel), which includes Anthrax Information, Public Health Emergency Preparedness and Response, as well as information for travelers with special needs for conditions such as a disability, pregnancy or HIV.

It is common sense to put health matters into the hands of medical experts. It can take a bit more ingenuity, however, to successfully protect your belongings.

In the office and on the road, you may be a bright and innovative corporate success. But, the next time you arrive in a strange city, try pretending you're a thief. Put your brain to work at how you could steal from an unsuspecting traveler.

The concept is not that radical. Once you accept the premise that robbery is a crime of opportunity, you can begin to defend against it. Be assured the professional thief will have even more tricks up his sleeve.

Richard Kahn, president of New York-based Kahn Travel Communications, was traveling in China with two cameras, one on loan from Kodak, when he was caught off guard.

"I was on a main street in a big shopping area in Beijing," he recalled. "I took a picture of three teenagers and then asked them to take mine. The guy handed the camera back and I put it in my side pocket. I was busy taking more photos, when suddenly, one of the teens pushed me from the front, the second knocked me down from behind and the third one took the camera out of my pocket and ran."

Fortunately, Kahn's story had a happy ending. Within two weeks, with the help of the Chinese consulate and a clear image of the culprits in his backup camera, the Kodak model was back in his hands.

A mugging in a public place could be more difficult to prevent than a burglary inside your lodgings. There, the onus of liability falls upon the operators of the hotel or motel, who are held to certain security standards—door locks, peepholes, telephones—to keep guests safe. It does not absolve individual travelers from responsibility, however.

A comprehensive brochure from Travel Smart Newsletter is entitled "Think Like a Thief & 49 Other Ways to Have a Safe & Healthy Trip."

"Thieves want only items with resale value: Laptops, handheld computers, cell phones, watches," the newsletter says.

It offers some other useful tips: Minimize losses by removing extra credit cards from your wallet. Carry more than one ID. Beware of connecting doors. And, book a room between the third and fifth floors, as rooms that open onto a garden are easy targets. Also, you can walk downstairs in case of a fire.

To help travelers evaluate security programs, some basic guidelines from the Foreseeable Risk Analysis Center can also be found at http://www.frac.com.

Kahn's camera theft in Beijing changed his thinking and made him more cautious in terms of possessions.

"I felt violated and upset," he admitted—but not enough to take out insurance.

To the contrary, Dr. Connor, whose extensive credentials include co-director of Medicine for Adventure Travel, says insurance is "always something to look into."

Depending on individual needs, business travelers may request to be covered in case of accidents or illness, business equipment failure and trip cancellation. A plan with optional war and terrorism coverage is also available. A general guide to understanding travel insurance, can be found at http://www.WorldTravelCenter.com.

The best place to go is your primary health care provider. Start by finding out if you are already covered, and to what extent.

(May 2002)

"Reprinted with permission. All rights reserved. © Reuters 2002."

21

Environment Control

The next time a weary corporate traveler gets a "Sorry, wrong number!" call at his hotel in the middle of the night, he might think back to how much—or whether—he tipped the bellman.

Still, in a world that's certain to stay uncertain, some things remain within our control. Unpleasant surprises, such as hotel staff retribution, an airplane seat near the toilets, crying babies, or falling victim to a crime in a foreign city, can be avoided.

Often, it begins at the time of booking a flight.

To avoid sitting for hours near a busy bathroom or galley, travelers can consult SeatGuru.com (http://SeatGuru.com). It provides color-coded cabin configurations—Green-Good Seat, Yellow-Be Aware and Red-Poor Seat—for more than a dozen major carriers, including American Airlines, British Airways, Continental, Delta, JetBlue, Qantas, SAS, United and Virgin Atlantic.

Comprehensive information on Internet access, legroom and limitation of seat recline is adapted to specific types of equipment—Airbus A320, Boeing 767-500, MD-88, and the smaller Embraer 145 or Canadair Regional Jet typically used on short trips.

To insure an atmosphere that's more conducive to concentration during a long flight, a business class passenger on a Cathay Pacific Airbus A330 should avoid center seats 11D and G as well as 19D and G by the galley; also 12A and C, and 12H and K next to the lavatories, according to the site.

In the all-coach class, 34-passenger Northwest Saab 340A, Row 1 seats C and D, with extra leg room, get SeatGuru's green light, while those with limited-recline in Row 5, in front of the emergency exits are rated Poor.

Cost control is another critical component of corporate travel today.

Cheapflights.com (http://www.cheapflights.com) entered the U.S. market in 2003 after Cheapflights.co.uk established itself as one of Britain's top 10 travel Web sites. It recently announced the addition of 15,000 business class deals through partnerships with specialists such as Access Fares and 1800 Fly Europe, and low-cost carriers Spirit and AirTran.

While many airlines compete by lowering fares, not all cater to corporate travelers. Song, for example, was promoting organic food items for "Frequent Criers"—words that strike fear in the hearts of many bona fide Frequent Fliers.

"Song does not have a specific program targeted to business travelers, but makes all efforts to accommodate a special seating request," a representative said. "There is a separate front section, if a business traveler wishes to be in a quieter area."

Urban noises create problems for people, and so does crying, says Dr. Charles Goodstein, a professor of psychiatry at New York University Medical Center.

Some temporary crying by a child in a strange environment is normal, but when it is prolonged "maybe airlines have to be more alert that there are travelers who don't think they should have to put up with this," Goodstein, a child and adolescent psychiatrist and psychoanalyst, said on the phone from his office in Tenafly, New Jersey.

It is incumbent on parents to find a way to soothe their children, he said. For flight crews, he suggests early intervention—offering assistance "within 5 minutes of crying."

In the meantime, Goodstein recommends that business travelers use earphones to try to block out as much sound as they can for the remainder of the flight.

On arrival, an unwelcome "wake-up" call in your hotel room can be averted by being familiar with rules governing gratuities, which do vary from country to country. Guides to help determine the appropriate tips for waiters, cabdrivers and porters around the world can be found at Web sites such as http://magellans.com.

Tipping etiquette in U.S. hotels, in Brazil and across most of Europe and the Middle East suggests that a bellman get $1 per bag, in contrast to places such as Argentina, Hungary, Japan and New Zealand, where no tipping is the norm.

Safe travel tips are shown in a short video aboard inbound London flights on Virgin Atlantic in conjunction with London Metropolitan Police. Practical advice that can be used when visiting any city includes safety and prevention practices such as exercising caution when using ATM machines and keeping an eye out for abandoned bags in public places.

Business executives tend to live out of a suitcase, and prefer traveling light.

Taking charge of their appearance—arriving wrinkle-free with clothes that fit the occasion and location—is made easier with advice excerpted from "Magellan's Passport to Compact Packing" by Jerry Camarillo Dunn at http://www.magellans.co.uk.

Some packing wisdom: To guard against dirt and wrinkles, put shoes in shoe bags and roll trousers from the cuff upward. Choose a medium to dark solid color for your main wardrobe pieces, take more tops than bottoms, and thin fabrics rather than bulky ones.

(November 2004)

"Reprinted with permission. All rights reserved. © Reuters 2004."

PART IV
AIR TIME

68   AWAY on BUSINESS

22

Sky-Level Gourmet Dining

At an altitude of 39,000 feet, taste buds lose sensitivity. With a traveler's ability to taste 33 percent gone, airline meals must be more robustly seasoned on the ground, and wines more aggressive on the palate.

Since no one consumes more airline food than business travelers, menu planning for repeat passengers is a constant challenge for airlines with long-haul routes.

"We are treating in-flight dining like in-flight entertainment, because the food has to work hard to keep passengers entertained," said James Boyd, spokesman for Singapore Airlines (www.singaporeair.com). "We need to satisfy a number of objectives. It's also a vehicle for creating a point of contact. The way a meal is presented creates an opportunity to interact with passengers."

To meet the taste challenge, carriers conduct costly and labor-intensive tests, some in kitchens that have a sealed room to replicate in-flight pressure and humidity conditions.

On long-distance flights, menus are changed regularly and tailored to ethnic preferences on given routes, which requires considerable research and attention to very specific guidelines.

"Meals must taste like this, look like this … exactly … according to detailed instructions," said Bob Ferguson, vice president of aircraft catering for Emirates in Dubai, who in March spent 180 hours traveling and sampling food.

Emirates (www.emirates.com) employs three food managers—Swiss, German and Arab chefs—to design menus for the international network.

"We do a tremendous amount of market research. Also a lot of self-analysis. We bring in samples without producers' knowledge and compare them with what we said we wanted," said Ferguson, himself a trained chef.

Singapore's food and beverage manager works with an international culinary panel—famous chefs of well-known restaurants—to produce an "insanely detailed" catering checklist of "every hors d'oeuvre, main course, cheese, beverage, fruit, baked goods and standard items, such as water, butter, salt and pepper," Boyd said.

"Each item is identified and numbered, with specified serving size or weight. Presentation should be perfect—down to the grill marks on a chicken breast or to the decision of whether berries are suspended in aspic or yogurt. Photos are taken of the dishes and circulated to galleys as a plating guide."

One dish was shipped back six times for re-crafting and perfecting the sauce color and drizzling pattern, he said.

As carriers cater to an ever-wider variety of cultures among their passengers, dietary laws or restrictions must also be observed.

Israeli carrier El Al, the world's largest kosher airline, serves only glat kosher meals, or food certified by rabbinical laws (www.elal.com).

"In Platinum Class, we combine very upscale food together with it being kosher. To give the feeling El Al is an Israeli carrier, there is lots of fruit and also vegetables, so people feel good after eating on board," said Nira Dror, vice president and general manager of El Al, North America.

Kosher service is up to 30 percent more expensive because separate kitchens, ovens, dishwashers and meat/dairy china are required. But El Al does not charge extra, she said.

"Menus are rotated monthly. During Jewish holidays, we add typical dishes, like honey cake for New Year, doughnuts for Hanukkah, matzos for Pesach," said Dror. "All food is freshly prepared. Our New York flight kitchen produces more than 15,000 meals a day."

"On Emirates, all meals are prepared in a manner that is suitable for Muslims," said Ferguson. "And, we have a very good selection of wines, which surprises people, who think they may not get any alcohol at all."

Meals with heart-friendly ingredients are served by Finnair (www.finnair.com) as part of an annual Finland-wide campaign to observe Heart Week. In April, Business Class passengers were served lime-marinated whitefish with dry rye bread, grilled chicken breast with mango sauce and wheat risotto, and black currant pastry.

British Airways' (www.britishairways.com) Sleeper Service for Club World passengers offers several dining options on selected overnight flights from North America and the Middle East to London's Heathrow Airport (www.britishairways.com).

In North America, the Terraces Lounge has a preflight selection of gourmet entrees, soups, salads and desserts, plus an extensive wine list. At New York's JFK airport, business travelers can choose a freshly cooked meal from the carving station or pasta bar.

On board, there is NightCap service of hot chocolate and warm cookies.

Individuals or groups on Blue Star private jets, www.bluestarjets.com, an increasingly popular method of corporate travel, get full bar and snack tray service and whatever meals they choose—from a restaurant or private caterer.

"We work around what customers want, as opposed to them getting what we serve," said Debbie Dickinson, vice president of marketing and public relations in New York.

(August 2004)

"Reprinted with permission. All rights reserved. © Reuters 2004."

23

Sky's the Limit for In-Flight Magazines

In-flight magazines were once the Rodney Dangerfields of publishing—they got no respect, as the comedian would say. And for good reason, as the publications had a reputation for being little more than empty travelogues stuffed into seat pockets to keep frequent fliers from going stir-crazy.

Now these highly marketable magazines, with guaranteed high circulation and a captive audience of affluent consumers, deliver content that is slick, smart, multicultural and often bilingual. Both readers and advertisers are taking notice.

"In-flight magazines are an editor's dream publication," said Howard Rombough, a London hotel executive and former in-flight magazine editor. "Unhindered by circulation ups and downs, the editorial team has an opportunity to create a lively, entertaining and informative read."

There are more than a hundred of them, with titles from the predictable "Altitude," "High Life" and "Wings" to the more imaginative "Hot!" and "Silkroad," to the straightforward-as-it-gets "Magazine."

Unlike newsstand publications, they are guaranteed to reach readers, each of whom is a potential customer for advertisers.

Frequent fliers are a dream demographic as they tend to be decision makers with purchasing power. The majority are 30 to 50 years old and traveling on business, receptive to new ideas and, as key consumers of goods and services, are searching for the best way to spend disposable income.

With hours of flight time ahead, they are usually relaxed. Sociologists have found that the level of absorption of the contents of an in-flight magazine is twice as high as that of other illustrated publications.

Aboard Magazines, publisher of a range of glossy magazines carried by 12 international Latin American airlines, claims to reach more than 75,000 potential clients every day with the pitch: "Dollar for dollar, passenger for passenger, no one brings you a more targeted advertising buy."

Inflight Magazines offers advertisers a potential global audience of nearly 75 million air travelers a month. MediaCourier, which sells advertising to air carriers from Finland, Ireland, Slovenia, Spain, Sweden, Turkey, Australia and the United Kingdom, among others, says it is able to reach "3,200,000 businessmen traveling in Europe."

As airlines encourage passengers to take magazines away with them, the advertising message is extended into homes.

To hold the attention of tired or jaded travelers, the importance of editorial content—energetic reporting on diverse topics from technology to sports to cooking—is not to be discounted.

Rombough, now public relations director of the luxury hotel One Aldwych, was until October 2002 the editor of "Voyager", the British Midland in-flight magazine, where he introduced a number of features that were considered unusual, including purchasing second rights to previously published short stories by well-known writers.

"Perhaps there was an outmoded perception that in-flight magazines simply write about the destinations flown to and by the particular airline, along with pretty photos," he said. "With Voyager, readers were delivered topical, issue-led features, like one reads in a Sunday newspaper magazine. Until budget cuts, Voyager carried short stories by respected authors such as Ruth Rendall, Hanif Kureishi and Martin Amis. It was a small way of keeping an undervalued literary form alive."

Another of Rombough's regular features was a two-page profile of a European politician by a national journalist, accompanied by a New Yorker magazine-style caricature.

Timely cultural and entertainment topics also attract reader interest with stories such as Singapore Airlines' cover "Lofty Ideals, turning architectural dreams into reality," and Delta's "Vintage L.A." theme.

In travel-related publications, strong photo essays have an indelible place such as in Garuda Indonesia's "Surf ... the final frontier, in search of the perfect wave," Southwest Airlines' "Winter Resort Guide," and Hawaiian Airlines' "South Seas Showbiz."

Often sharing the seat-pocket with airline magazines are business- or shopping-oriented companion publications.

British Airways' "High Life," whose cover blurb states "Winner: Best Travel and Leisure Magazine," and its accompanying "Business Life" have received high marks from frequent fliers. And the carrier's research shows its "Shopping the World" brochure has an even higher readership than its in-flight magazine.

Israeli flag carrier El Al magazine editor, Ronit Heber, serves passengers' interests in two very different languages. The English pages of "Atmosphere" appear in the accustomed front-to-back fashion, while the Hebrew pages start at the back and read toward the front.

Another editor meeting the communications challenge is Stuart Lawrence at Cathay Pacific's magazine, where advertisements, stories and captions appear in English as well as Chinese.

"The business is more positive than it seems to be from the headlines," said Inflight Sales Group CEO Jean-Marcel Rouff at the Airline and Supplier Conference 2002 held in Geneva.

(December 2002)

"Reprinted with permission. All rights reserved. © Reuters 2002."

24

Airport Hotels Get Image Makeover

Airport hotels have battled an image problem for years. Seen as chaotic and devoid of stylish decor or decent service, they have been regarded as the aviation equivalent of a truck stop—suitable only for basic rest and refueling.

Now, with spacious suites, high-tech conference facilities, revolving restaurants and modern fitness clubs, the hospitality industry's ugly duckling is emerging as a swan.

Air travel is projected to increase. Add a steady volume of international and transit passengers, supplemented by the normal flight delays or cancellations, and aided in no small part by the strict security measures brought about by the attacks of Sept. 11, 2001, airport hotels are reaping the benefits.

"9/11 had a big impact on airport hotels. They are very popular today," said Carlton Werner, the general manager of the deluxe Radisson Hotel at Los Angeles International Airport. "With tremendous changes in security, even international travelers, since 9/11, are feeling a lot better about staying close to the airport."

Hotel executives concur that the sense of security extends from within the airport to the hotel itself and being able to walk to the terminals saves time and energy.

"Many business people are opting to come into the airport area the night before to save a couple of hours of sleep," Werner said. And even though the hotel at LAX is between four runways—two on each side—they have no trouble sleeping. "The windows are double pane and have a 5-inch separation. We never, never hear a complaint about noise."

Local business travelers also are taking advantage of the Park, Stay and Fly program offered by Radisson, Werner said. "Before an early flight, they come in, spend the night and leave their car at the hotel. Parking for a week earns them additional gold points and when they return, the auto is right there."

Out-of-towners have the cost-saving option of not having to rent a car. With the hotel only 20 minutes from downtown Los Angeles, they can take a cab or limo, which costs the same as rental, with the added benefit or avoiding the headaches of driving in freeway traffic.

The first airport hotel in Greece, the 345-room Sofitel Athens Airport, opened in November 2001. Across the street from the main terminal building, it has two executive floors with separate reception and meeting rooms.

"It's like business class in an airplane," said George Stavrou, sales and marketing director for Sofitel's parent group Accor hotels, adding that 82 percent of guests are from the corporate segment.

"With the newest technology and construction materials, there is absolutely no noise in the hotel," Stavrou explained. "Our clients say they cannot believe they are in the airport."

As services evolve to meet today's needs, executives find that airport hotels may even have an advantage. Most are on a main road to the city center, have easy access to ticketing and baggage areas, shuttle service to terminals, rental car agencies and comfortable lounges for airplane or people watching.

For global business, London's Heathrow has more international flights than any other airport in the world, said Steve Knight, business travel development executive for VisitBritain in New York. "With people coming from all over the world ... they are used to dealing with quicker turnaround."

It can also be more cost effective.

"Budgets still aren't what they once were and that is paramount at the moment," Knight said, adding that most major chains are represented on nearby Bath Road, including Radisson Edwardian, Renaissance and Hilton, which is connected to Heathrow's Terminal 4.

With high turnover come more frequent improvements, says Trisha Molina, general manager of Holiday Inn Express Miami Airport in Florida. "Most airport hotels are busy with short-term guests, so you can expect to find renovations. Guests will encounter new carpets and furniture, updated televisions with more satellite channels and more food and beverage selections."

The Starwood-managed Westin Detroit Metropolitan Airport connects to Edward H. McNamara/Northwest World Gateway terminal, said Scott Stinebaugh, the hotel's sales and marketing director. Business travelers can land, attend a meeting and depart the same day, or spend the night in a deluxe room if they choose.

In the greater New York area, Marriott has more than 1,400 guest rooms near Newark Liberty International Airport.

The Tampa Airport Marriott, with CK's Revolving Rooftop Restaurant, is inside Tampa International Airport, recognized by travel information guide OAG (www.oag.com), as one of the Top Five in the world. "You can literally step off the plane, make your way to the main terminal and walk directly into the hotel's lobby," said Matthew Carroll, manager, North American communications for Marriott International.

The Renaissance Toronto Airport hotel, with an 18-hole golf course, is just 1-1/2 blocks from Toronto Airport, which handles 80 percent of all arrivals into Canada.

(August 2003)

"Reprinted with permission. All rights reserved. © Reuters 2003."

25

Seat-Pocket Gift-Shopping

For busy corporate travelers who can't spare valuable time standing on line in a crowded store, shopping for a last-minute gift is just an arm's length away—in the aircraft seat pocket in front of them.

"In the rush of traveling, you don't always manage to get everything done," said Ben Delaney, president of CyberEdge information services, in Oakland, California.

"It's great when I realize I was supposed to bring something for the host where I'm going, or a gift for my wife," said Delaney, who has bought "perfume, jewelry and gadgety things" from in-flight boutiques during his travels to Europe and Asia.

Long-haul carriers have a vast selection, often 100 or more pages, of duty-free merchandise, a veritable Who's Who or Fortune 500 list of internationally known brands—Sony, Clinique, Gaultier, Zegna, Steiff—of handheld computers, cameras, cosmetics, perfume, silk or leather goods and, of course, toys.

"Some items are really quite fine and some more plebeian," said retailer David Cully, CEO of Blue Tulip, whose stores in Princeton and Marlton, New Jersey, and Paoli, Pennsylvania, "revolve around gifts for personal occasions" in people's lives. "The branded gifts have the most appeal."

Names with global recognition give foreign-flag carriers an opportunity to showcase their own designers, like British Airways' inclusion of Stella McCartney and Paul Smith items, classic Burberry ties and scarves, plus memorabilia from Concorde, which made its last trans-Atlantic supersonic flight in October 2003.

Germany's Lufthansa puts forth Hugo Boss, Jil Sander, Porsche and Braun brands, and Austrian Airlines its selection of Swarovski crystal bracelets, rings and necklaces.

"You are really trading on brand recognition and the quality that is associated with that brand," said Cully, whose travels this year took him to Germany, Atlanta and Dallas.

Duty-free shopping guides are printed by vendors, who also handle inventory. They cater mostly to sophisticated adults, as illustrated by Alitalia's abbondanza of high-profile names such as Armani, Versace, Fendi, Ferragamo and Dolce & Gabbana.

A choice of more than 30 designer fragrances for women and a dozen for men is available in Air France's La Boutique, as are Longchamp leather goods and Fauchon chocolates.

Scandinavian-made products such as Denmark's Georg Jensen silver, Swedish crystal and Finland's colorful Marimekko products take the spotlight in the pages of SAS's Flightshop.

There is no tax, so the customer's total cost tends to be lower than in luxury stores, but "in that kind of environment, price is less of an issue than convenience," Cully contends.

Often-bored frequent flyers may get a lift from the cheeky twist that Virgin Atlantic's Retail Therapy magazine gives to generally predictably named product sections, by using titles such as Sniff Sniff, Yum Yum, Glug Glug, Gimme Gimme and Bling Bling. And, for the edgiest, steamiest layouts, they can reach for a copy of TAP Air Portugal's bilingual On Air magazine.

On trans-Pacific routes, passengers can buy in-flight or via mail order. Such products as Singapore Girl silk scarves and batik travel bags are available from Singapore Airlines' KrisShop. JAL's duty-free and mail-order catalog sells Mikimoto pearls and Japanese brewer Suntory's 12-year-old malt whisky. Smokers will find Chunghwa cigarettes on China Southern, the largest airline in the People's Republic of China.

"It's a little more interesting at the international level," said Cully. "On domestic trips, the flights are shorter and I am often preoccupied with other things."

Nonetheless, the very successful SkyMall, the largest U.S. in-flight and mail-order catalog company, has more than 20 partners—American Airlines, United, Delta, Continental and Northwest among them. Its Holiday 2003 issue has 252 pages of gift ideas in 11 categories—from Apparel and Automotive to Pets and Office—available from more than 10 featured stores such as Hammacher Schlemmer, Magellans and Sharper Image.

Everybody wins, says aviation consultant Peter Klaus.

"It's a great thing for the airlines. Say you have one flight a day 365 days a year, averaging sales of $1,000 or above. With 20 flights a day, it adds up," said New York-based Klaus. "If you derive a 20 percent or 30 percent profit without overhead, it's not difficult to figure out that it is a good thing all around—good service for the passenger and profitable for the airlines and the duty-free companies."

(December 2003)

"Reprinted with permission. All rights reserved. © Reuters 2003."

26

Life after Concorde

No more sipping champagne while hurtling at twice the speed of sound, or curvature-of-the-Earth views from an altitude of 60,000 feet. No more "beating the sun" on a London-to-New York flight.

The pampered elite of business travelers must bid farewell to Concorde forever, as British Airways' sleek and elegant needle-nosed beauty makes its final commercial flight on October 24, after 27 years of service.

But, enough supersonic nostalgia. Executives are a practical lot.

"Am I sad it's going away? Yes. Is it the end of the world? No," said frequent Concorde flyer David Grayson, managing director of Auerbach Grayson, a New York-based global stock-broking firm.

"My profile as a Concorde user is a bit atypical," said the executive, whose first supersonic flight was more than 25 years ago. "I use it to travel beyond London, to shorten time and make myself more productive. Concorde flies London to New York in less than 3-1/2 hours, compared with nearly eight hours for a subsonic flight.

"The biggest plus was Asia with practically no jetlag. I could work all day long in Bangkok, fly overnight and sleep, land in London at 5:30, shower at the airport, put on a clean suit, get on Concorde and be in the office by 10:30 New York time, ready for another day's work," said Grayson, who plans to go on using the supersonic plane as long as it is available.

"It becomes a bit of a private club. There are some people I see only on Concorde. You get to know crew and ground staff," he said.

Cabin Crew member Adele Sinton knows the customers—captains of industry, CEOs and directors of global banks—by name, and is familiar with their particular likes and dislikes.

"I'm aware of their preferred style of service, and able to anticipate their needs," she said from her home in England.

"Two of our most frequent Concorde customers prefer the red burgundy to the claret. So, when I know that they are flying with me, I make sure the red burgundy is always at their disposal—without them having to ask for it," Sinton said.

The 6-foot-6-inch Grayson in future plans to fly British Airways' First Class because "their beds are that length."

"In a way, for BA, it's a good move," he said. "With business travel being down as much as it is, it will help them to fill the First Class seats."

Business charters are not a practical alternative for him, Grayson said, because "most of my travel is solo and generally I am going to different locations all the time."

Airplane manufacturers and corporate jet services, however, view Concorde's demise as an opportunity for expansion and have declared open season on soon-to-be-former passengers.

At the Paris Air Show, NetJets Europe brashly announced the start later this year of trans-Atlantic service. Their slogan: "You flew Concorde—now it's time for an upgrade."

Some major carriers already offer corporate jet service—such as Lufthansa's PrivatAir and Delta AirElite. Airbus Corporate Jet deliveries are expected to more than double.

While corporate jets do not fly supersonic, they do shorten waiting times and are more cost-effective.

NetJets, a unit of Warren Buffett's Berkshire Hathaway, allows companies or individuals to buy part of a plane, giving them the right to fly for a set number of hours per year. It plans to fly 35-to 15-seat Gulfstream jets between small private airports outside London and the New York area.

Virgin Atlantic came close to using Gulfstreams on the London-New York route before supersonic service was reintroduced in 2001, after the crash of Air France Concorde outside Paris in July 2000 temporarily grounded the aircraft.

Now, Virgin is wooing the elite passengers of Concorde and First Class with its Upper Class Suite, which consists of a reclining leather seat, a place to sit and dine opposite your partner, the "longest fully flat bed in the world with a proper mattress," onboard bar and private massage room—all at the same price other carriers charge for business class.

In June, Air France's Concorde made its last flight Paris-to-Washington, D.C. The aircraft was presented to the Smithsonian Institution's National Air and Space Museum for display at the Steven F. Udvar-Hazy Center, adjacent to Washington Dulles International Airport in northern Virginia.

(July 2003)

"Reprinted with permission. All rights reserved. © Reuters 2003."

Part V
HOTELS

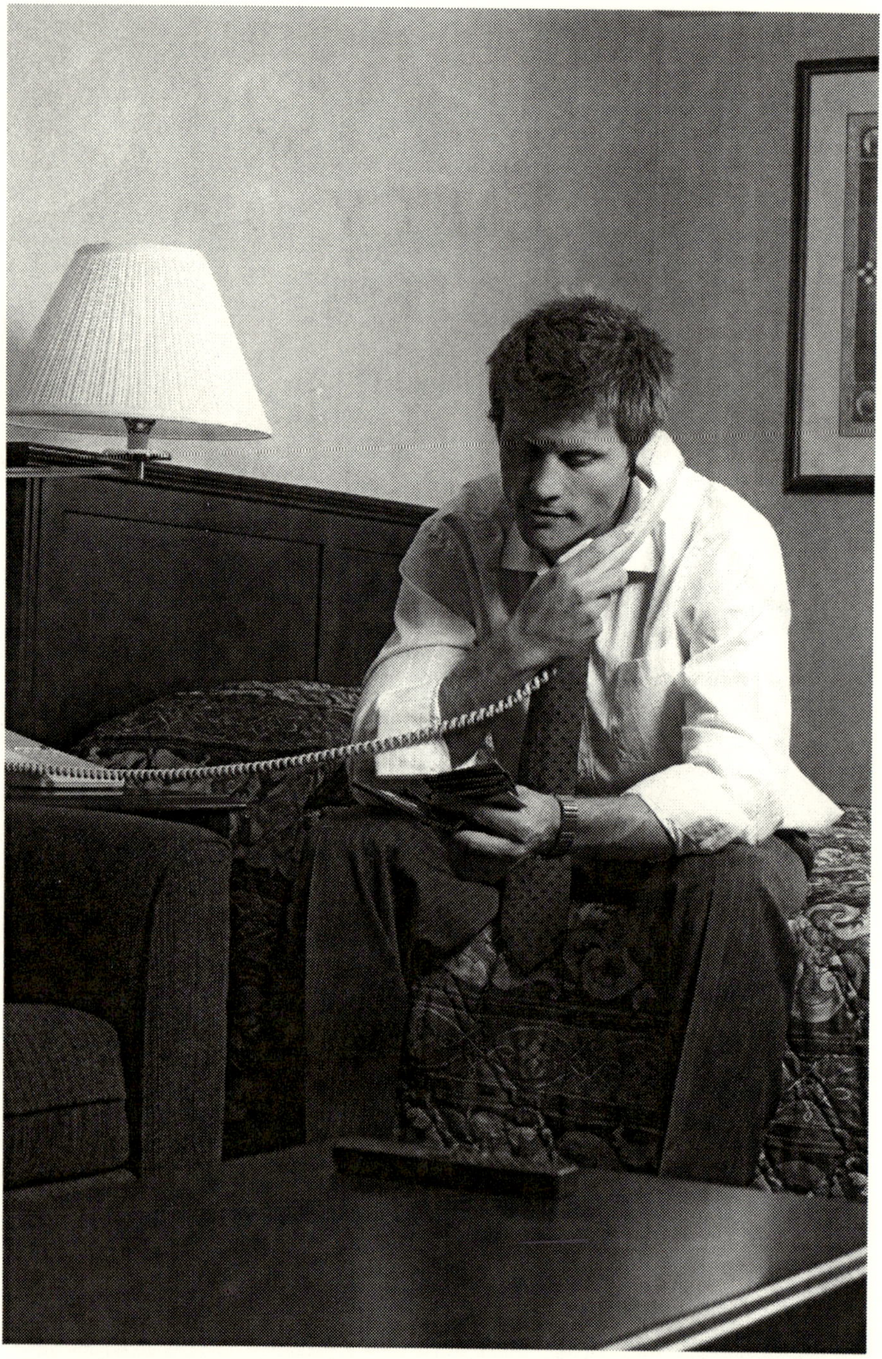

27

Kept Awake by Bells and Whistles?

Hotels rooms aren't just for sleeping anymore. They're hubs of high-technomania equipped with broadband and wireless connections, 42-inch plasma screens, video-conferencing units, ergonomic chairs and e-butlers. It's enough to keep a weary traveler awake all night.

Increasingly dependent on corporate business, hotels all over the world are competing to find ways of bringing the high-productivity concept to the next level.

But, will building a smarter room necessarily produce a more intelligent guest? Or, does the pressure to deliver results rest evenly with both sides.

"Obviously the hotels wouldn't be adding amenities unless there was some sort of demand from the travelers themselves," says stress specialist Dr. Elizabeth Carll. "It's just a matter of knowing when to stop."

"No one is expected to work 24 hours a day ... Everyone needs some time out, even on a business trip," said Carll, a Long Island, New York-based psychologist and workplace consultant.

To keep business travel a positive experience, hotels are blending low-tech comforts of home with a high-tech environment.

Sheraton Smart Rooms, for example, created a relaxing work environment that allows guests to work effectively within a bedroom suite which doubles as a fully equipped private office that includes a desk, an adjustable chair, multi-channel TV, radio, minibar, fax/printer and modem outlet.

Industry estimates show that business travelers account for 80 percent of extended-stay—five or more consecutive nights—guests nationwide. While increasingly computer-savvy, not all are comfortable with technology overload.

A national survey conducted by a travel magazine found that in-room coffee makers, easy-to-reach dataports and ironing boards topped the list of preferred amenities for business travelers. And a poll of hotel general managers in 2000 ranked voicemail, Internet access and coffeemakers in the top three.

Meeting the challenge of integrating art and technology is Le Meridien Minneapolis, adjacent to the city's high-energy Block E Development, the equivalent of New York's Times Square. The hotel is a short walk through the city's climate-controlled Skywalks to high-end shops such as Saks Fifth Avenue and Neiman Marcus, just across from the sports arena, and near the business and theater districts.

"We couldn't have landed a better or more visible spot to showcase Le Meridien's cutting-edge Art + Tech product," said Juergen Bartels, CEO of Le Meridien Hotels & Resorts.

The rooms have modern furniture, beds specially engineered for comfort, a multimedia entertainment system, 42-inch plasma TV screens, and high-speed Internet access.

The concept was conceived by Bartels, based on his philosophy that the upscale traveler not only demands substance and comfort, but is also looking for something different. Traditional landmark properties such as Le Meridien's Grosvenor House in London also partially incorporated the concept.

London's Art Deco Dorchester's state-of-the-art 42-inch plasma screens are concealed in wooden cabinets to retain the hotel's English country house style, while offering e-butler and business services.

The Ritz-Carlton's South American property is located in the fashionable Las Condes area of Santiago, the Chilean capital. Club Level rooms, accessible by elevator key, offer upscale amenities, along with a level of comfort and privacy. Food and beverages are available in the Club lounge throughout the day, as are the services of a multilingual concierge staff.

"Santiago offers the perfect location to enter a cosmopolitan destination while providing convenient access to recreation and cultural attractions in and around the city," says Simon Cooper, president and CEO of The Ritz-Carlton Hotel Company LLC.

Gentler needs may gain preference as baby boomers continue to age and, in addition to work support, require amenities such as Yoga tapes, libraries or even access to a hotel doctor.

The Lake Austin Spa Resort in Texas features prominent U.S. physicians and experts in health, nutrition, behavioral science and exercise training in its "Fresh Start to Fitness" program, with interactive sessions and problem-solving seminars (http://www.lakeaustin.com).

Marriott International worked with spa consultant Suzie Somers to create a distinctive atmosphere at its first branded spa, Revive, at the JW Marriott Desert Ridge Resort & Spa in Phoenix, Arizona.

Marriott's plans also included reinventing its Courtyard by Marriott brand, the "hotel designed by business travelers for business travelers," by adding The Market, a 24-hour pantry with "grab-and-go food"—freshly prepared sandwiches and salads, beer, wine, frozen desserts and snacks available for business travelers whether they check in at midnight or are just brainstorming into the wee hours.

For frequent travelers to New York, the Hilton Club (http://www.thehiltonclub.com) offers members a home-away-from-home in a studio or one-bedroom suite on two premier floors of the Hilton Hotel in the heart of midtown Manhattan. Development of the project, which combines vacation ownership privileges with the advantages of a full-service hotel, was overseen by Parisian born Antoine Dagot, president and CEO for Hilton Grand Vacations Company, LLC, with headquarters in Orlando, Florida.

Some places even encourage writing on the walls.

Embassy Suites Hotels was testing a type of room, the Creativity Suite, designed to stimulate business travelers' creativity—and, by extension, their productivity. The suites have sectional sofas that can easily be rearranged into "thought-provoking positions," and grease boards, complete with a box of crayons, which travelers can put to use if struck by an idea, even while taking a shower. Similar rooms were being planned in Chicago and Los Angeles.

Products that can help keep work-weary travelers' dispositions sunny include lamps and handheld stress monitors.

"Hotels nowadays are outfitting rooms with bright light units that are five to 10 times brighter than normal home office lighting. That intensity is therapeutic and can be used to adjust sleep style," said light therapy expert Neal Owens, who has been involved with clinical research for 20 years and is president and founder of The SunBox Company in Gaithersburg, Maryland.

And Canadian manufacturer of handheld biofeedback equipment, Thought Technology Ltd, helps put executives in touch with their level of stress, so they can manage it better. Changes in body function are transformed into a signal, such as a tone or meter reading; a rising tone indicates increased tension.

Lawrence Klein, vice president of the Montreal-based company, said the devices, used by hotel spas, are "about to be re-computerized to be plugged into PCs."

(January 2003)

"Reprinted with permission. All rights reserved. © Reuters 2003."

28

Recipe for Success

Cancel the limo. Put down the dining guides and leave your overcoat in the closet. A power breakfast or lavish business dinner is just an elevator ride away.

In venues from Palm Beach to Paris—bustling financial districts, oceanfront resorts and busy harbors—hotels with internationally acclaimed on-site restaurants are attracting a loyal corporate clientele.

At New York's Millennium Broadway, executives from publishing, finance and the entertainment industry frequently meet at Restaurant Charlotte, where Chef Aleksandra Parada is known for health-conscious low-carb dishes like Chilean sea bass and Mediterranean chicken.

"We follow 60 percent trend and 40 percent personal favorites," said Parada, a University of Warsaw graduate who puts no geographic boundaries on food sources, serving salmon from Scotland, New Zealand meats, and South American fruits and vegetables.

On Florida's Atlantic coast, southeastern regional produce drives menu choices for Palm Beach Four Seasons' acclaimed Chef Hubert Des Marais, whose simply named Restaurant has a Five-Diamond, four-star rating and "a huge number" of local, regional, European and South American repeat guests.

"It's not just quality of food, china or service, which is always evolving. To be a player, you need to keep pushing. It's a prestige thing," said Des Marais, a frequent traveler to Asia, Europe and New York, who conducts tours of his tropical herb and rare fruit garden and greenhouse.

Achieving balance falls to Harry Gorstayn, general manager at Four Seasons, which offers 24-hour business services and an annual Wine and Food Classic.

"It's more than the menu. It's the whole evening, the flowers, the surroundings. Creating atmosphere is a financial burden as well," said Gorstayn, who also puts high value on interacting with guests, calling it 80 percent of his job.

In Dallas, The Adolphus hotel's French Room ranks among the 25 best in the world. "The majority of clientele fly in from all over—Asia, France and England.

George Bush, father and son, have eaten here," said Executive Chef William Koval.

"I don't get into the cutting-edge stuff," the plain-spoken, internationally acclaimed New Englander said. "My trend is not to follow a trend."

Most chefs and managers see the hotel-restaurant combination as a good thing. Yannick Alleno's le Meurice in the Hotel Meurice in Paris was awarded two stars from Guide Michelin. In general, the restaurant gets more international exposure because in-house guests from all over the world are introduced to it.

Hyatt International has an enviable crop of chefs creating menus for the discerning taste buds of world travelers.

Chef Sandro Gamba of Park Hyatt Chicago's NoMi grew up with the aroma of oven-fresh pastry in historic St. Avold in northern France. "My father baked croissants and my mother sold them."

He likes to keep things simple while staying connected. "I don't go on the floor for applause. I go to make people feel like they are in my house," he said, maintaining that the home kitchen is the "greatest laboratory for cooks."

Concept, tradition and innovation are all part of the success formula.

"Concepts are there for a reason—they work," said New York Grill Chef Matthew Crabbe at Park Hyatt Tokyo. "Being part of a large hotel chain, attention must be paid to the company's standards, control systems and work ethic."

Tradition is a passion for Marco Perez, executive sous chef at Park Hyatt Milano and resident chef of The Park. Basing 80 percent of his cuisine on personal favorites, he studies old cookbooks and adapts recipes to his own "modern Italian" style. "I also like to research unusual marriages of ingredients, such as natural yogurts or flowers."

Grand Hyatt Tokyo's German-born Chef Josef Budde's sweet tooth led him to launch an afternoon dessert buffet at the Hong Kong property, where Marco Avitabile, a German-born Italian, now works his own culinary wonders.

On the marketing side, Singaporean Jack Aw Yong, executive chef at Grand Hyatt Beijing and 17-year Hyatt veteran, notes: "We consider guest expectations, from a hybrid analysis of international and local guests" leading to a draft menu and trials using local staff and management—expatriates from various countries. A sales analysis follows to further sharpen the menu.

At InterContinental Hong Kong, Laurent Andre, executive chef of SPOON by Alain Ducasse, reports to the high-profile partnership of the hotel and Alain Ducasse Group. "There are demands to meet the extremely high expectations of both," he says.

If there is a down-side to the hotel-restaurant combination, it's fierce competition with free-standing restaurants, said Charlie Sheil, Millennium Broadway's food and beverage director. "We are looking at getting a separate entrance."

(October 2004)

"Reprinted with permission. All rights reserved. © Reuters 2004."

29

Strange Bedfellows

Sleeping in the same bed as Madonna, Bill Clinton, Victoria Beckham, Derek Jeter, the Vanderbilts, Sean Connery or Madeleine Albright is a claim to fame shared by many well-traveled corporate executives.

OK, so maybe it wasn't on the same night.

Hotels all over the world glory in stories about guests past and present—royalty, rock stars, politicians, athletes, gangsters, ghosts and the English poet who carried on a love affair with the hotel owner's wife.

While the tales may be used as promotional enticement, there is a self-imposed line many hotels will not cross.

"Gossip and discretion do not mix," said London-based Andrew Warren, managing director of Conde Nast Johansens Ltd., publisher of guides to hotels and country houses throughout Europe, North America, the Caribbean and the Middle East. "Great hotels remain stubbornly silent regarding the identity and antics of celebrity guests. To break this rule is commercial suicide."

There is a Gold Book that guests can sign at the Hotel Ritz Madrid in Spain, where the World Bank, OPEC and Sony have held private meetings.

"If a guest writes in it, we consider it public," said Anton Kung, the general manager. "Mr. (Jacques) Chirac stayed in the Royal Suite after the (French presidential) elections and used the office to meet with government officials. David Beckham celebrated New Year here."

Kung emphasized that it is a balance, and client comfort is paramount. "This type of hotel lives on publicity, but also discretion," he said.

The exception, says Johansens' Warren, might come a reasonable time after a celebrity is deceased and his antics or indiscretions may safely be recalled.

"For many, this adds a sense of mischief to the idea of being in the same place or bedroom, even a century later," said Warren, who admits he felt "rather special" during a stay in Cottage No. 10 at Round Hill in Jamaica when told that Mr. and Mrs. John F. Kennedy honeymooned there.

In 1813 England, the notoriety of Swynford Paddocks country hotel in Newmarket, Cambridgeshire, was assured by a passionate affair between the poet Lord Byron and the owner's wife.

More strange bedfellows, centuries apart, help shape the legend at Ynyshir Hall in Wales, which has hosted Queen Victoria, Richard Gere and television's "Antiques Roadshow."

Joining in the fantasy—be it romance or power—can relieve the drudgery of life on the road.

Rooms 104/105 at the Dorchester hotel were the London base for U.S. General Dwight D. Eisenhower during World War II. In what is now the Eisenhower Suite, Allied generals planned the June 6, 1944, Normandy Invasion. Other notable guests have included Nelson Mandela, Mikhail Gorbachev and Arnold Schwarzenegger.

The $2,850-a-night two-story Everglades Suite at The Biltmore Hotel Miami, in Coral Gables, has seen former Presidents Clinton and Carlos Menem of Argentina, and fashion CEO Tommy Hilfiger and his family. "Many dignitaries and celebrities request that suite, popularly known as 'The Al Capone Suite,'" said Ivonne Perez-Suarez, media relations manager. "It has its own butler service."

Sports-minded CEOs are drawn to the Centerfield Suite at New York's Radisson Lexington Hotel, where Yankees baseball legend Joe DiMaggio lived for 18 years. For part of that time, DiMaggio shared the terrace view of midtown Manhattan, a living room, dining area, bedroom, master bath and kitchenette with his equally famous wife, Marilyn Monroe.

The Edgewater in Seattle, a local conference favorite, gained prominence more than four decades ago when the Beatles went fishing from its windows.

Washington D.C. hotels are rife with stories of political and romantic scandal. Captured on Four Seasons' lobby video, which the Georgetown hotel refused to release, was a spat between Donald Trump and then fiancee Marla Maples, who threw her engagement ring at him.

In the heart of Paris, travelers can share suite memories with Sarah Jessica Parker's "Sex and the City" character Carrie, who spent the final two episodes at the luxurious Plaza Athenee contemplating her future.

The French Riviera, best known for the Cannes Film Festival, is also important for commerce. The Carlton InterContinental caters to both industries and has named suites for Elton John, Sean Connery, Uma Thurman, Sophia Loren and Alain Delon.

Asia travelers gravitate to the Park Hyatt Tokyo, a frequent choice of actress-director Sofia Coppola, who made it the setting of her Academy Award-winning movie "Lost in Translation."

"While contemporary celebrity guests mostly wish to remain invisible, they still might of course become part of the hotel folklore in years to come," said Warren.

(August 2004)

"Reprinted with permission. All rights reserved. © Reuters 2004."

30

Expanding Your Horizons

If traveling is an education, corporate frequent flyers hold an advanced degree. Still, for those who want to keep learning, hotels along the way provide opportunities in subjects as diverse as French cooking, Arabic lessons or Zen art.

Lower Manhattan's Millenium Hilton, where more than half of the guests are business travelers, has themed cooking and wine tasting classes taught by Executive Chef Joseph Verde in its Church & Dey restaurant.

"It's interactive and casual," said Verde, also food and beverage director at the hotel. "At the end, they eat what we show them how to cook."

Themes have included the American heartland—veal stew with dumplings–as well as the Northeast, Pennsylvania Dutch and Christmas in New York.

Using the premise that seasonal produce makes the best cuisine, the Rib Room & Oyster Bar at The Carlton Tower hotel in London's Knightsbridge has offered "Seasonal Cooking Classes" with Executive Chef Simon Young and BBC Radio's "Veg Man" Greg Wallace. One year, the October specialty was Atlantic cod, with Norfolk turkey and winter vegetables in December.

In Paris, Sofitel guests can jump the queue, normally up to six months long, to enroll in a four-hour class at the world renowned Lenotre Cooking School, with instruction in French.

Ne parlez pas francais? The Royal Garden Hotel in London offers executive travelers privately tutored lessons in 25 languages. The program, developed in conjunction with UK-based Professional Language Studies, covers a range of learning, from intensive study to refresher courses to basic phrases in Arabic, Cantonese, Dutch, Greek, Norwegian, Polish, Thai and Turkish, among others.

The Park Hyatt Hamburg has an alliance with the nearby Goethe Institute to teach German, while Brazil's Grand Hyatt Sao Paulo refers long-stay guests or newly assigned foreign executives to a Portuguese language teacher.

For those who don't want to waste a minute, Virgin Atlantic has teamed with Linguaphone, which has courses in 30 languages in 80 countries, to introduce

Spanish for English speakers and English for Spanish speakers. "Passengers can learn basic phrases or brush up on fluent conversation, which is perfect for business or leisure travelers," says Rebecca Smith, the airline's manager of acquisitions and publishing. "We hope to expand the selection to include Chinese and Japanese to link with our routes to the Far East."

Others may choose the cross-cultural appeal of sports.

Austria's Hotel Schloss Fuschl near Salzburg has a private lake where guests can learn from resident master fishermen how to use the angling rod, then proceed to the castle kitchen, where chef Thomas Walkensteiner will help them create a delicious dish with their catch.

Golf lessons are available on the 9-hole course at the hotel, a 15th-century hunting lodge and summer residence of archbishops.

In Vienna, corporate history buffs at Hotel Imperial or Hotel Bristol can arrange horse-drawn carriage or architectural guided walking tours of the 2,000-year-old city that was the center of the Habsburg Empire for 600 years.

Artistic expression serves a dual purpose as an acknowledged form of stress relief.

Georgia O'Keeffe-style inspiration is strong at Fechin Inn in Taos. Besides golfing on New Mexico's No. 3 rated course or fly-fishing in the Rio Grande, guests can take part in the "Artist-in-Residence" workshop.

"Zen of Art" sessions are held poolside at The Spa at Camelback Inn in Scottsdale, Arizona. "When guests realize how simple it is to paint the Zen way, they say, 'I can do this at home ... I feel more connected with myself,'" says teacher Lu Bellamak, many of whose pupils hold high-stress jobs. Her "Zen Meditation" class involves "living in the moment, sitting in silence and letting go of the many thoughts that roll through our minds every minute."

Miraval, Life In Balance in the foothills of the Santa Catalina Mountains in southern Arizona's Sonoran Desert, has personalized programs to minimize and eliminate stress, and also to stop smoking.

In-room coaching and meditation sessions are a part of each month-long stay at New York's Regency Hotel.

But sometimes overworked travelers just want to have fun.

The Westin Maui's Hawaiian cultural classes offer hula dancing and the art of making leis, said Bridgette Okamoto, public relations manager.

And New York's Gansevoort, along with the Scratch DJ Academy, has provided DJ lessons in the hotel's conference rooms.

True sybarites can savor a three-day international wine symposium in Colorado's Vail Valley, presented by Park Hyatt Beaver Creek and distributor Southern Wine and Spirits.

(September 2004)

"Reprinted with permission. All rights reserved. © Reuters 2004."

31

When Guests Speak, Hotels Listen

When corporate guests ask for something, smart hotel managers get it.

At the end of every trip, business travelers have an opportunity to create their own wish list by filling out a questionnaire that will help hotels serve them better during future stays.

Topics cover basic efficiency and courtesy of staff—room service, doorman, concierge or cashier—as well as more specific concerns like shower pressure, room decorations or CD selections.

"It's a key indicator of how you are doing on a daily basis," said Anthony Lee, general manager of The Connaught (www.theconnaught.com) in London's Mayfair district. He follows up each questionnaire with a personal note thanking the guest for filling it in. While 85 percent of respondents say services are "excellent," Lee said he tends to focus on the lesser ratings to see which areas need attention.

"I really appreciate it," Lee said. "I give them the feeling they are not being picky, but doing us a favor for telling us what we can do to improve our home."

Carefully considered guest comments have resulted in butlers being equipped with wireless pagers, shaving their response times to between 20 and 25 seconds, and bottle stoppers that keep champagne bubbly for three days.

From a marketing perspective, business travelers are a constant pool of survey respondents who help hotel management road-test, alter, scrap or fine-tune their repertoire.

At Trump International Hotel & Tower at the corner of New York's Central Park (www.trumpintl.com) guests call the shots. Their suggestions resulted in the removal of desks from suite bedrooms and the installation of illuminated make-up mirrors.

"When the hotel opened, we had beautiful bathtub caddies with amenities," said Melisa Novick, director of sales and marketing. "Though they were visually appealing, guests did not find them useful and suggested we remove them, so we did."

The Four Seasons' Spa in Palm Beach, Florida, (www.fourseasons.com/palmbeach/) often "test-drives" new products, such as Xela aroma sticks.

"We put it out for guests to try and, if it's popular, we'll stock it," said Manager Colin Clark. "It has to be available virtually exclusive to us and, on average, we change and update products every eight months."

The Four Seasons Gift Shop stocks a variety of items used within the hotel—iced tea glasses in the Ocean Bistro, martini glasses in The Living Room lounge/piano bar (a big seller at about $75 per four-piece set) and sterling silver salt-and-pepper shakers in The Restaurant (about $150). Also, bathrobes, bedding and orchids—all chosen based on frequent guest requests.

A brochure lists the most popular items available for sale—mattresses, pillows, duvets, bathrobes, spa products, the L'Occitane in-room bath amenity line, and even the showerhead, Clark said.

One of the most extensive questionnaires in the industry is claimed by London's Athenaeum Hotels and Apartments (www.athenaeumhotel.com/). It covers room temperature, decor, audio sound and TV picture quality. A detailed history of repeat guests keeps track of profession, birthday, hobbies, favorite type of music, dietary requirements and drinks preferences.

The hotel spends 100,000 pounds ($185,520) per annum on its guest amenity program, said General Manager Jonathan Critchard.

"We encourage feedback from our guests and are cognizant that we need to deliver on our promises to deliver their preferences," said Critchard. All within reason, of course. "While guests now have more of a selection of protein foods at breakfast," he said with a smile, "… we were unable to accommodate a request for a swimming pool on the roof of our hotel."

Sofitel Worldwide hotels use an in-room comment card as well as a more detailed e-mailed survey requesting customer feedback on staff friendliness, room ambience and quality of meals or bar service, said Scott Wiseman, vice president of marketing for the chain's operator, Accor North America.

The Sofitel brand's trademark "l'art de vivre a la francaise" (French art of living) translates into fresh flowers, Roger & Gallet soaps, MYBed featherbeds and a new shopping catalog, SoBoutique (http://www.SoBoutique.com), that lists items from decorative objects to gourmet edibles and bath products.

Pampered guests are happy guests and, for hotels that pay attention to their concerns, they are repeat customers.

(November 2002)

"Reprinted with permission. All rights reserved. © Reuters 2002."

32

Vying for Rooms With Donkeys and Elephants

In 2004, a U.S. presidential election year, with thousands of political conventioneers heading for Boston and New York looking for places to hang their party hats, there was concern that corporate travelers would find rooms in short supply.

Hotel space was at a premium as the host cities for the Democratic and Republican national conventions prepared to welcome tens of thousands of visitors—delegates, alternates, dignitaries, support staff, and foreign and domestic press.

Special events such as this call for special preparations.

"All hotels want to take care of their frequent customers, especially coming out of a tough three-year cycle for the hotel industry," said Joe McInerney, president and CEO of the American Hotel and Lodging Association in Washington.

"When they bid for a national convention, cities look at any major conferences or anything else they have on their books and make sure there is no major conflict," he said.

Boston, a first-time host, put on a month-long celebration starting on Independence Day, July 4, to set the stage for the Democratic National Convention, July 26–29, and the nomination of Massachusetts Sen. John Kerry and his choice of running mate at the 19,000-seat Fleet Center.

The Democrats reserved 80 percent of the rooms in selected hotels, with 20 percent set aside for corporate and leisure guests. The Greater Boston Convention & Visitors Bureau (www.bostonusa.com) was not concerned about a shortage of rooms, with 68 Boston and Cambridge hotels and 80 more hotels in neighboring suburbs.

The luxury XV Beacon Hotel was holding 50 percent of its rooms for loyal guests, said William Sander, the general manager. "We were extremely proactive in contacting all our corporate clients well in advance to ensure they had accommodation if they planned on being in town that week."

In the run-up to the convention, all visitors could enjoy special festivals, concerts, Shakespeare performances and patriotic reminders of Boston's role in American history—the Boston Tea Party, Sons of Liberty, the Revolutionary War, and the abolitionist, suffragette and Civil Rights movements.

Ritz-Carlton hotels set the mood with topiaries shaped like donkeys (symbol of the Democrats), patriotic music, and red, white and blue embroidered pillowcases. Restaurant menus were offering Brahmin Buffet Brunch, Kerry Berry Cobbler and (Vermont) Governor (Howard) Dean's "I Scream" Dessert. The Jer-ne bar will serve Teresa Heinz Kerry Tomato Martinis.

The Langham Hotel's "Road to Washington" package included red, white and blue cookies, a "Boston Presidential" cocktail made with Stoli Razberi Vodka, Blue Curacao and cranberry juice, a copy of "Profiles in Courage" by John F. Kennedy, and two tickets for a Boston Trolley tour or a Harbor Cruise.

New York City's choice of dates for the Republican National Convention—Labor Day weekend—meant that corporate traffic was even less likely to be affected there.

"It is a traditionally uncongested period, when millions of New Yorkers are away from the city," said Paul Browne, New York Police Department deputy commissioner for public information. "That will counterbalance the number of people who are here for the RNC, for business or to protest."

New York, a veteran of five political conventions—all Democratic, until this one—was expecting, by some estimates, a quarter of a million demonstrators.

But security operations would not interfere with day-to-day life except around Madison Square Garden, the convention site, Browne said.

For the hospitality industry, the convention is a bonanza.

"This is the pinnacle, the Super Bowl, of event housing," says Ray Vastola, president of Travel Planners Inc., the official housing coordinator for the Republicans.

Some hotels imposed a minimum length-of-stay requirement, not uncommon for major citywide events.

"We expect the end of August/beginning of September to be extremely busy," said Mark Pardue, general manager at The Stanhope Park Hyatt. "We have been encouraging our frequent guests to book early while there is still availability."

Treats awaiting guests at Ritz-Carlton hotels, where some rooms were set aside for corporate travelers, included yellow roses of Texas, the home state of President George W. Bush; chocolate elephants and peanuts; and lights projecting a silhouette of an elephant—the Republican Party symbol—in the night sky over Central Park.

NYC & Company (www.nycvisit.com), a nonprofit group that promotes New York tourism worldwide, invited visitors to "Come Early and Stay Late." It extended "Convention rates" at selected hotels, with "great discounts and special offers" to cultural and sightseeing attractions, retailers, theaters and restaurants.

Penny-watchers could save time, money and aggravation with "The $5 Lunch" by Eddie Sugarman and Jeffrey Shubart, a book listing 50 spots in the Times Square area to grab a quick and affordable bite.

(May 2004)

"Reprinted with permission. All rights reserved. © Reuters 2004."

33

It's Beginning to Look a Lot Like Christmas

In the weeks leading up to the holidays, business trips still take corporate executives to the usual destinations, but the venues themselves are transformed with a festive flair.

As busy travelers strive to balance the demands of work and the desire to spend time with friends and family, their comfort and well-being rests in the hands of the hospitality industry.

"The first two weeks in December are the highest business travel weeks of the year, as well as the most challenging," said Michael Pitstick, vice president of sales and marketing for Carlson Hotels Americas.

"We made a cognizant decision to maintain our hotel decorating policy because we feel it really does provide a home environment for our business traveler," he said. "We did not cut back on budgets at all. For example, in the main lobby of our Radisson Hotel South in Bloomington, Minnesota, we annually put up a 30-by 8-foot gingerbread display."

As most hostelries pull out all the stops, their task is made easier by the fact that the very trappings of the holiday season—the colors, scents and sounds—serve as a natural antidote to loneliness and gloom.

Colors are known to heighten the senses, and the traditional Christmas red, symbolizing energy and passion, offset by the calm and harmony that green conveys, may even portend a better chance for success in deal making. Carols and hymns have a soothing effect on frazzled nerves, and the glow of candlelight flickering off shimmery tinsel helps brighten the too-short winter days.

Spirits are lifted on takeoff for passengers on Israeli and Scandinavian flag carriers and the innovative Virgin Atlantic.

El Al serves traditional treats—sufganiot (Hanukkah doughnuts) and latkes (potato pancakes)—on all flights throughout the celebration of Hanukkah.

Stockholm-bound passengers booked on certain December SAS flights originating in Chicago and Newark awaken after the longest night of the year to the musical Lucia procession. The "Queen of Light" in a white gown with a crown of candles in her hair walks along the aisles, accompanied by white-clad attendants and boys wearing cone-shaped hats decorated with stars.

"The Lucia celebration is still part of the in-air festivities—with typical Swedish carols, Lucia, attendants and star boys, serving mulled wine, Christmas pastry and ginger cookies," said Robert Segerman, assistant product manager of SAS product Management Inflight Business Division.

Virgin menus in December reflect traditional holiday dishes, with roast turkey replacing Coq au Vin for Economy class passengers, who also get Mincemeat Pie at afternoon tea, and an added treat of Christmas pudding with brandy sauce or cream for Upper Class guests.

To make weary or homesick travelers feel instantly welcome, hotels concentrate on arrival areas.

Carols on the lawn, a roaring fire in the hearth and twinkling lights on a towering tree greet guests at the White Barn Inn in the woods of Kennebunkport, Maine. Horse-drawn sleigh rides, hand-painted tree ornaments, Christmas pudding in every room and a welcome bottle of wine complete an atmosphere of family warmth and values. (http://www.whitebarninn.com)

The romance of Christmas past is recaptured at Circa 1886, an elegant carriage house restaurant on the grounds of the 21-room Wentworth Mansion in Charleston, South Carolina. The Charles Dickens' "A Christmas Carol" holiday dinner program includes a dramatic reading of the Dickens classic, and guests may ride in a horse-drawn carriage to three historic inns as part of the "progressive Dinner Hotel Package." (http://www.wentworthmansion.com)

In Saskatchewan, Canada, 9-foot toy soldiers guard the entrance of the Radisson Plaza Hotel, where on the first Tuesday of every December, guests are treated to a gala reception that includes the Regina Symphony and food and drink from around the world. (http://www.hotelsask.com)

Christmas season in London officially begins in mid-November with the switching on of the Regent Street lights and a party on the closed-off world famous shopping street.

Centrally located 51 Buckingham Gate Luxury Suites and Apartments, have personal butlers to make sure your stay goes off without a hitch. The Christmas Magic package includes a traditional dinner and tickets to the theater and select tourist attractions. (http://www.51-buckinghamgate.com)

A "White Christmas" concert in Royal Albert Hall is the highlight of a stay at the Vanderbilt Hotel. (http://www.radissonedwardian.com)

Travelers anxious to fill the hours before boarding their flight home can go shopping for Christmas presents.

In New York, five Madison Avenue blocks, from 58th to 63rd streets, are designated the official Crystal District and include world's leading crystal makers Baccarat, Daum, Lalique, Steuben and Swarovski.

Philadelphia's Radisson Plaza-Warwick Hotel has a GO! Shopping package from late November through January, that includes a shopping bag with gifts, brochures and discount offers from 30 local retailers.

Berlin's Spandau Market opens in late November and, with about 400 booths, is one of the largest Christmas markets in Germany. Organized weekend programs combine shopping with music, gourmet, fashion and art. (http://www.berlin-tourist-information.de)

If the idea of being away from home and family is simply more than you can bear, the only thing left to do is to change your travel plans.

The National Parenting Association suggests pointing out technological alternatives such as videoconferencing; finding someone else to take your place, or asking your company to revise its corporate travel policy to eliminate Saturday night stay-overs and traveling on business during the holidays.

More than two-thirds of frequent business travelers say they try to make fewer trips during the holiday season between Thanksgiving and New Year, compared with the rest of the year, according to a survey which also revealed that about a third of business travelers who have a child at home travel every week.

Meeting away-on-business parents half way is the Royal Garden Hotel in London's Kensington High Street, which stocks a range of children's books for every age for guests to borrow. Mom or Dad can pick up a copy of "The Cat in the Hat," "Harry Potter" or "Mother Goose" and phone home with a bedtime story (http://www.royalgardenhotel.co.uk).

(November 2002)

"Reprinted with permission. All rights reserved. © Reuters 2002."

PART VI
SEPTEMBER 11, 2001

110   AWAY on BUSINESS

34

Taking It One Step at a Time

The violent destruction of the World Trade Center was a direct hit at the heart of international commerce. The fallout will touch every business traveler whose job involves getting on a plane dozens of times a year.

For them and their employers, the first order of business now is to address the crisis, calm their fears and look to the future.

"These are terrible hours," begins a letter to the staff at SEI Investments Co. from Chairman and CEO Alfred P. West. "While it is difficult to think of much else than the catastrophe and its aftermath, we have to be concerned about our clients and each other."

West, who heads the global investment services firm based in the Philadelphia suburb of Oaks, Pennsylvania, offered guidelines to SEI's more than 1,000 employees in 25 offices in 11 countries.

They include: "Please do not put yourself in harm's way. Please do whatever is necessary to fulfill your family obligations. If you are out of the office, please stay in closer touch than usual."

"SEI is working on expanding accommodations," but "if all else fails, feel free to bring your children to the office," the letter continues, taking a decidedly humanitarian approach, putting people before profits.

"We receive frequent security updates from AmexOne, which makes bookings for our staff, who travel quite extensively. At the moment we have people in from London, and there is an international conference planned in our Paris office next week, but we are taking things one day at a time," said Sabrina Y. White, marketing director for SEI Wealth Network.

The company also offers easy access to any developments via its Web site, http://www.SEIC.com.

Italian-born Claudio Zancani, the director of technical sales for Atlanta-based software company Red Celsius, takes 40 to 50 business trips a year. He has a pilot's license with an instrument rating and is the co-owner of a single-engine Beechcraft Bonanza V-tail, which he uses to fly for pleasure.

Admittedly "still dealing with the details" of the recent tragedy, Zancani said: "What's needed now are new rules that differentiate between the 'traditional' hijacking—where demands are made for money, to call attention to a cause, or to be taken to a certain destination—and the 'new terrorism' which is mass destruction."

He said the recent hijackings would have been impossible if there was no way for the pilot to leave the cockpit. "We need rules that make the cockpit inaccessible. That is the only way the airplane will stay an airplane and not become a weapon in an act of homicide ... an act of war."

"We spend billions on building rockets ... they spend $1,000 on airfare and maybe $10,000 learning how to fly an airplane. And, if you look at the total cost, they spend nothing to make the biggest impact," Zancani said.

Beyond issues of safety, being stranded far from home can be very stressful for travelers, a situation that many hotels overseas are having to address.

Graham Bamford, general manager of The Royal Garden Hotel, near Kensington Palace in London, is no stranger to dealing with out-of-the-ordinary events. When Princess Diana died, the crowds lining up to place flowers at the gates of the palace, Diana's residence, stretched through the park and past the entrance of the hotel.

The main thing to be done for his American guests is to make them comfortable and "provide them with good communication via the hotel's sophisticated Internet services," Bamford said. "We must act with great sensitivity and empathy. What's called for here is compassion, not panic."

No one has been booted out or is being overcharged.

"I have to think how I would feel if I were away from home and my country was attacked," said Bamford, who also reported having "an eerie experience. A male caller left a voice message for me with a 212 area code. But when I tried to ring back, the number was gone."

Now, perhaps more than ever before, "people have to be concerned about where they meet when they travel on business," said Steve Norcliffe, commercial director of The Queen Elizabeth II Conference Centre in London.

The seven-story venue overlooking Westminster Abbey and the Houses of Parliament was built like a fortress by the British government to provide the world's highest levels of security for top-level government meetings. Its exceptional security systems and state of-the-art technology soon came to the attention of corporate meeting planners, who now use it extensively.

"There are many reasons for a company to choose a secure facility. People use this center because they worry about terror attacks, industrial espionage and demonstrations, among other things," said Norcliffe.

But the serious traveler won't be deterred. From his office in the Watchung Mountains in Union County, New Jersey, just 25 minutes from New York City, Tim Benford, president of Benford Associates, Inc., a public relations firm, said he has heard from all his clients in Europe, the Pacific, South America, and the Caribbean. All of them expressed concern for the victims and offered support.

"Up to this point, not a single one has raised the question of travel safety or its potential impact on business," he said. "I have two overseas trips, as well as domestic flights, scheduled in the months ahead and I intend to do them.

"Hell will freeze over before I let my freedom of travel be compromised by madmen and heartless killers," said Benford, who is also author of "Pearl Harbor Amazing Facts!"—a collection of odd, unusual vignettes and anecdotes, and about 40 pre-attack warnings.

(September 2001)

"Reprinted with permission. All rights reserved. © Reuters 2001."

35

De-Accessorizing Long Flights

Business travelers who need to arrive at their destination clean-shaven and well-coiffed may have to rethink their grooming strategies.

Heightened security at U.S. airports because of the Sept. 11 attacks has resulted in the confiscation of previously innocuous items such as hairspray, nail clippers, disposable razors and even glass perfume bottles.

But with some advance planning, and a little help from the airlines, the fastidious can still reach their destination refreshed and ready to take a meeting.

Business class travelers to Italy will see only minor changes, says Marta-Marie Lotti, director of press and public relations for Alitalia.

"We have deleted pens as well as razors from our Magnifica Class amenities kit, and removed men's and women's grooming kits from our in-flight boutique. If a passenger wants to shave in the morning, a flight attendant will provide a razor," said Lotti, who has seen "everything from a nail file to a miniature Empire State Building" confiscated by airport security.

At Japan Airlines, "the only change we've had to make is to substitute plastic utensils for cutlery and discontinue distributing razors," said Irene Jackson, Manager, Public Relations The Americas. "But plastic safety razors will be available upon request … No JAL passenger shall go hairy."

Jeff Kriendler, North America public relations officer for the Brazilian airline Varig, said: "We've swapped cutlery for plastic knives and forks. Nothing in our amenities kits was deemed dangerous, and, as far as freshening up, there's an airport arrivals lounge with showers passengers can use."

Other traveling professionals, such as hair stylists, are more directly affected, as the items now being confiscated from hand-luggage involve the tools of their trade which could be lethal in the wrong hands.

"The heightened security is obviously presenting a challenge," said Rick Haylor, international creative director for John Frieda Salons. "A stylist's kit is very expensive, very specialized and very personal. Mid-range scissors alone are priced at around $1,000. Normally we would never let the kit out of our sight."

"Can you imagine being flown to do an ad job or editorial shoot and not being able to start because your luggage has not turned up?" said Haylor. "The unfortunate part is that there's no standard procedure, each country and airline are handling their security differently, so we don't really know what to expect."

As far as appearance, "the biggest challenge on long-haul flights is that the hair gets flattened." To avoid that, Haylor advises having your hair blown out before you fly and using a thickening lotion at the roots. Just before arrival simply rub the fingers at the roots of the hair, and the lotion will be reactivated, giving your hair volume.

Ken Cranford, a stylist at the Stephen Knoll salon on New York's Madison Avenue—whose clients include Jordan's Queen Noor and supermodel Cindy Crawford—is planning a trip to the South and never travels without his professional kit.

"I am going to mail it ahead. It's more valuable to me than to anyone else, and I won't risk losing it," Cranford said.

But rules are rules, and even being the manager of a professional baseball team is no exception. New York Mets' manager Bobby Valentine turned over a "small multi-purpose tool" after it was picked up by an airport X-ray machine.

There are still other seasoned business travelers, however, who simply fail to see what all the fuss is about.

Retired airline executive Morris Simoncelli has traveled to Japan "at least 80 times" and says he never had a problem and doesn't expect that to change.

"I honestly don't recall that I've ever shaved on an airplane, even on a flight as long as 13 or more hours. Flights to Japan arrive in the evening and you can go to your hotel to relax and freshen up. If I felt I had to shave, I'd take an electric razor," he said.

Gillian Craig, director of the British Antiques Dealers Association Fair held annually in London, welcomes the restrictions.

"In this day and age, regardless of recent events, it is not necessary to travel with scissors, razors and tweezers! I have never seen people doing their nails or plucking their eyebrows on a flight. And the queues for the loo make you realize it is selfish to linger in them!" she said, taking the unflappable English approach. "For those that need a shave, the airlines carry wash kits. And if this is no longer allowed, then we will have to see some unshaven faces getting off some planes.

"If all this leads to less hand baggage, so much the better," Craig concluded. "Passengers can be loaded and off-loaded much faster, and the faster the movement of passengers through the interminable terminals, the better."

(September 2001)

"Reprinted with permission. All rights reserved. © Reuters 2001."

36

Air Travelers Look to the Heavens

Business travelers in the habit of making a beeline for the cocktail bar nearest their departure gate, may now be more likely to seek spiritual refreshment in the airport chapel.

Stressed-out and often sleep-deprived, they are generally more vulnerable to "anticipatory anxiety" in the times after September 11 that psychologists have labeled "the new normalcy." Indeed, since the destruction of New York's World Trade Center claimed victims from 86 nations around the world, a new lexicon of psych-speak has intruded into our daily lives.

Another term gaining currency, they say, is "the God factor."

"I've noticed a considerable increase in the number of people looking for the chapel and coming in to say a prayer. I'd say it's almost double," said Father James Devine, of Our Lady of the Skies, the Catholic chapel inside New York JFK International Airport's Terminal 4. "I've seen business travelers here. I've talked to them after the service and they've appreciated the opportunity to say a prayer before they fly out."

Anticipatory anxiety—the fear of what could occur—is the reason some people have avoided flying altogether, according to trauma psychologist Robert R. Butterworth, Ph.D., who, in the days following the attacks, became a familiar face on channels such as CNN, CBS, NBC and Fox.

He advised that it's important for people not to get swept up in rumors of doom.

"The reality is that we're not hiding in our homes, but starting to get back on planes, and the stock market has stabilized," Butterworth said.

And in the world's busiest airports, amid the tumult there are islands of calm—interfaith chapels or meditation rooms. Many of them are attended by clergy and are ready to meet passengers' spiritual needs 24 hours a day, seven days a week.

For example:

- Chicago's O'Hare Airport Chapel, located on the Mezzanine in Terminal 2, was described by a traveler as "an oasis of spiritual refreshment in the midst of one of the world's busiest transportation points". Supported solely by donations, it is open 24 hours a day for prayer and/or meditation, with a chaplain available for personal emergencies.

- At Hartsfield Atlanta International, a chaplain is on duty Monday through Sunday 8 a.m. to 6 p.m., while the chapel remains open 24 hours a day.

Interfaith chapels can also be found in the airports of other major U.S. hub cities such as Boston, Denver, Dallas-Forth Worth, Miami and St. Louis.

In Canada, counseling and crisis intervention are provided for passengers at Toronto's Lester B. Pearson International, and multi-denominational religious services are held at the chapels in each of the airport's three terminals.

Overseas, airports in the Scandinavian capitals of Stockholm, Oslo and Copenhagen all have chapels, called quiet rooms, for various religions, said Anders Bjorck, director of Marketing Communications for Scandinavian Airlines System SAS. "They are places where you can worship or just sit down and rest, or seek guidance if you wish."

"It is important to note, however, that they are outside the customs barrier," he said. "A departing passenger must, therefore, make time to stop before going through security and arriving passengers can pause, if they wish, after clearing immigration and customs."

Individual airlines, as ever, offer special lounge privileges to their business class passengers.

British Airways' Terraces lounge at JFK reflects nine separate concepts, including an indoor garden, library, a phone-free zone, dimmed lighting, soft "tranquility" sound effects and carpeting to absorb excess noise.

When it comes to the need for meditation or a shot of courage, however, the habits of some frequent travelers remain unchanged.

"To be honest, the events of September 11 have had very little impact on my decisions to travel," said frequent flyer Steve Fox, who as a principal at Cap Gemini Ernst & Young, has logged as many as 100,000 air miles in the course of a year. "I get to the airport a little bit earlier and bring my own bag of peanuts."

Fox finds the extra security measures are mainly for show. "The real risks of air travel now are with baggage handlers, caterers, mechanics, and cleaning staff."

Joe Ojubai, managing director for SEI Investments (Europe), says he has made about 10 trans-Atlantic trips since the terror attacks and for him it's all about having fewer options and less time to do anything—period. "I've found it takes a lot longer to prepare to travel these days. I go to the airport much earlier and all my time is taken up by security checks—and not much left for anything else."

Back in JFK's Terminal 4, where four chapels reside side by side, Rabbi Paul Hait admits it's difficult to say with any certainty whether the number of worshipers in the international synagogue has increased. But proportionally—judging from the guest book registration—it's a different story.

"There has been an overall decrease of travelers since September 11. But in relation to that, the proportion of travelers who now frequent our place of worship must be at least 90 percent. It's a very high percentage," he said.

"I've noticed there are men who are flying to Israel even though they live in the U.S. They have faith and confidence both in God and in the pilots, maintenance crews and all those responsible for the safety and security of passengers. If they are a little more anxious than they were a couple of months ago, it's hard to measure," Rabbi Hait said.

(November 2001)

"Reprinted with permission. All rights reserved. © Reuters 2001."

37

Corporate Bookings Reflect 9-11

Empty chairs and silent microphones are likely to be the norm at many U.S. hotel conference facilities in the days around September 11, 2002—a time that travel industry experts say will be set aside for reflection and remembrance.

"I'm hearing in New York that there will be very little business travel that week. You'll probably see some of the same in Washington, D.C.," said Laila Rach, associate dean, Tisch Center for Hospitality, Travel and Tourism Administration at the New York University School of Continuing Education.

The reasons, she said, were twofold—a fear of traveling combined with wanting to remember the tragedy last year when hijackers took over four airliners, slamming two into the World Trade Center's twin towers and one into the U.S. Pentagon. The fourth jet crashed in a western Pennsylvania field, putting the final toll at nearly 3,000 lives.

On either side of the first anniversary of the tragedy, the number of scheduled flights have been cut, and the expectation is that more discount fares will be offered as people remain reluctant to travel.

"From a business travel standpoint, research can be rather difficult more than seven to 14 days in advance," said Keith Jackson, vice president of finance and operations for North America, at Rosenbluth International, a corporate travel management services provider. "Our meetings group has seen a downturn in conference activity for the week of 9/11."

"While there is no moratorium or mandate to not travel, the reality is that people will handle this on their own and probably steer away from that week," Jackson said from his Philadelphia office. "We are seeing a lull, but after that the expectation is on the rise."

"Groups are very obviously avoiding September 11," said Michelle Payer, director of public relations for the Ritz-Carlton hotels of Miami. "Normally a Wednesday is a very busy day, but that day is about remembrance.

"But, after that day bookings at the Ritz-Carlton Key Biscayne (about 10 minutes from downtown Miami) take a huge jump," Payer said. "We have 18 groups arriving in the balance of the month—three of them on the 13th. They're coming from all over the country—quite a few from the Northeast; some from the Midwest, West Coast, and even England."

In the heart of New York's Times Square and theater district, at least one hotel will be bustling with activity.

"The Marriott Marquis will be busy during the week of 9/11, with 1,000 rooms booked for a group attending a major convention," said Daren Kingi, director of market sales NYC Marriott Hotels. "The booking was made about 24 months ago and the group made the decision to go ahead with their plans."

With the long Labor Day weekend preceding the days leading up to September 11, a general slowing in business-related activity is neither unexpected, nor surprising.

"The month of September is a bit skewed this year because religious holidays are also impacting some of our business travel," Kingi said. "But we expect the Marquis to come in at around 91 percent (occupancy)." He added that occupancy for the hotel group's other properties around the city will probably come in at the "upper 70s or lower 80 percent."

It is a positive sign for The Marriott group, which lost "an entire building"—the 820-room Marriott World Trade Center—as a result of the terror attacks.

Remembrances are still in the planning stages.

"Our objective is to observe the day in a tasteful way without seeming self-promotional or self-serving," said Kathy Duffy in the public relations department for NYC Marriott hotels. She said a dedication ceremony is planned at Marriott headquarters in Bethesda, Maryland, involving the flag that flew outside the Marriott World Trade Center.

Rosenbluth, ranked among Fortune magazine's 100 Best Companies to Work for in America, also plans to take a very humanistic approach to the anniversary.

"With 3,000-plus people stranded as a result of the tragedy, our staffers stayed on the phones and worked through the night last year to accommodate them. We think it's going to be a time of reflection for that group, and we will respect that," Jackson said.

Weak travel demand around the anniversary this year has caused several U.S. airlines and international air carriers to reduce flight schedules. Major U.S. hub-and-spoke carriers, however, will need to maintain their regular schedules.

In September, the demand for air travel was expected to be so weak that even Southwest Airlines, the only one to report a profit for each quarter since the attacks, was not expecting to make money that month.

Earlier this month, a lack of reservations prompted British Airways to cancel 26 of 78 trans-Atlantic flights for September 11. Air France also canceled some flights and Virgin Atlantic said bookings were down.

(August 2002)

"Reprinted with permission. All rights reserved. © Reuters 2002."

Part VII
War

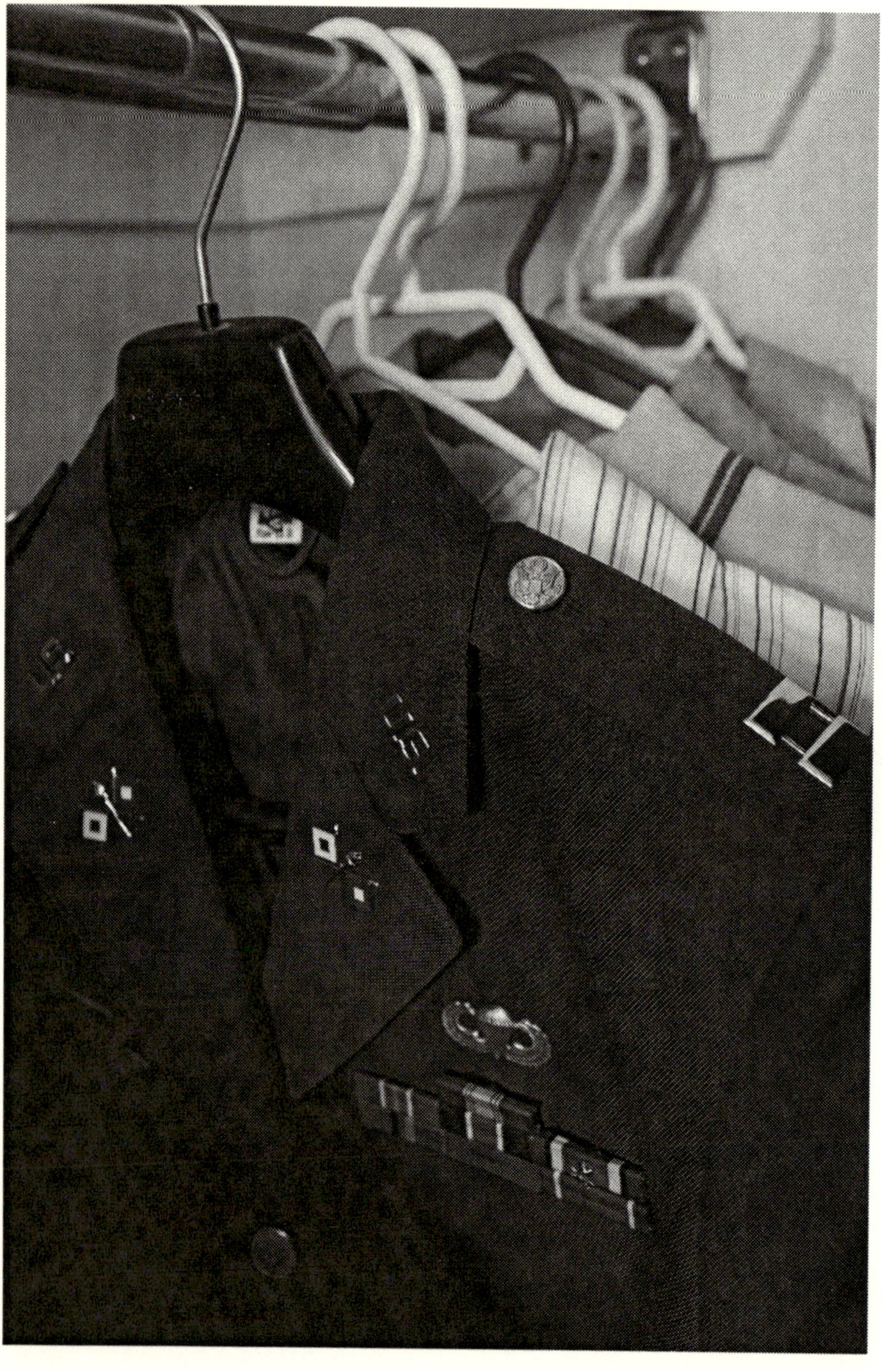

38

Another Battle in the War on Stress

Corporate business travelers, already stressed to the limit, have yet another layer of anxiety to deal with—the mounting threat of war on Iraq.

Juggling workload and jetlag with fear and uncertainty can be tricky, but it's not impossible if you plan ahead, experts say.

Since 9/11, "there has been an entire turnaround with the thought process of seasoned business travelers," said Boston-based personal security consultant Robert Siciliano. "I'm sure the majority have a plan of action and would leap to restrain a potential hijacker if necessary," he said, referring to the tragic flight that crashed in a Pennsylvania field after passengers overpowered their hijackers.

"Be aware; know your options. Don't jump to conclusions, and pay attention to general safety rules," said Siciliano, whose Web site (http://www.SafeTravelSecurity.com) offers security tips in 16 categories including Anti-Hijacking, ID Theft, Personal Safety and Safe Travel, beginning with: "Pay attention to the way you walk, your posture, facial expressions and eye contact. Know what is going on 50 to 100 feet around your body at all times."

"As far as stress, pick up a book or a magazine. Think happy thoughts," said the author of "The Safety Minute."

Sociologist and individual consultant Ginni Graham Scott suggests using self-talk or mental imagery as a way for travelers to put themselves in a state of calm.

"Tell yourself 'Relax ... calm down,' snap your fingers or get a picture in your mind to refocus yourself," said Scott, who holds a law degree and has written 35 books, including "Resolving Conflict," "The Empowered Mind" and "The Creative Traveler."

"The idea is to redirect your attention to something you can do something about. The first step is to get yourself really calm. Start by resolving your emotions, use reason to understand the situation, then bring in your intuition to come up with alternatives," advises Scott, who has conducted workshops and seminars for companies such as State Farm Insurance and a Nissan auto dealership.

People who conduct their lives on the run are constantly adjusting to new eating and sleeping patterns and often prone to exhaustion, which brings a decreased capacity for physical and mental work. Proper diet, therefore, is also essential.

"When you're traveling, you get out of sync with your normal schedule. A lot of the way you feel has to do with feeding yourself on a regular basis, or about every four hours," said Mary Kaye Sawyer-Morse, San Antonio, Texas-based registered dietitian with a PhD in health promotion.

Sawyer-Morse, who is on a plane almost every week, carries a small plastic bag of dried fruit—raisins, apricots and pineapple—and, on domestic flights, a couple of fresh apples.

"Don't do too much caffeine," she cautioned. "It magnifies the stress response, making it more difficult to think clearly."

Unresolved feelings of hopelessness are known to increase cortisol, a stress hormone that may affect your immune system, so it helps to think positively.

"These are anxious times for our country, fraught with elements of uncertainty and fear—emotions that will affect everyone differently," says Peter G. Burki, chief executive of LifeCare, Inc., a privately owned employee benefits organization that provides clients with counselors and educational materials 24 hours a day, seven days a week, to get people psychologically and practically prepared for disaster.

In the first six months of 2002, the number of U.S. health and sports clubs grew by just over 2 percent, attributed in part to Americans' struggle to deal with stress, according to the International Health, Racquet and Sportsclub Association.

While American stress levels remain high, the current situation is a global concern, where individuals have their own ways of dealing with everyday pressures.

A 1990s' study to establish how Europeans cope with stress, found that the most popular way to unwind was a hot bath or shower, followed by reading and watching TV. The French were the most energetic, with 68 percent taking some form of exercise, compared with 49 percent of Britons, Spaniards (48 percent) and Italians (47 percent). The British preferred drinking alcohol to unwind (43 percent), more than the Spanish or Italians (both 8 percent).

A most unusual way of alleviating stress has been demonstrated by Russian businessmen, who role-play as street beggars in purposely stained, smelly clothing and cosmetically applied bruises. After an hour, they clean up and meet in an expensive restaurant, and whoever has managed to beg the most money collects a token sum from his comrades.

For hotels around the world, travelers' needs remain the highest priority.

With nine properties in London's West End, Radisson Edwardian has linked its security camera system directly to the Metropolitan Police offering around-the-clock surveillance to improve the safety of the area for its guests.

Hotel Plaza Athenee in Paris has culturally customized minibars—so that Japanese guests have green tea and Japanese beers, while minibars for Middle-Eastern guests are emptied of alcohol and stocked with extra chocolate, nuts and sodas.

Eye masks and sports drinks are found in Hyatt International hotels from India to Australia.

On-edge travelers can take a page from "The New American Bartender's Guide" by John J. Poister. Goodnight Sweetheart Hot Milk Punch is one of more than 2,300 recipes in the book, which includes bartenders' secrets, house specialties from the world's great bars and more than 50 drinks "sans spirits."

"Go easy on alcohol," warns Sawyer-Morse. "A little is fine, but too much can make you restless and give your body toxins to deal with when you're trying to keep things on an even keel."

To make sure travel plans go smoothly, it's important to be well-informed. For current worldwide caution public announcements, travelers can visit the U.S. Department of State Web site at http://travel.state.gov and consult the department's Consular Information Sheet for specific concerns on any given country.

(February 2003)

"Reprinted with permission. All rights reserved. © Reuters 2003."

39

For Concierge, it's Business as Usual

In the tense weeks leading up to the war in Iraq, the most frequent requests from travelers were for restaurant reservations and theater tickets, not gas masks, escape routes or bottled water, say concierge staff at some of the world's top hotels.

From New York to London to Shanghai, a random survey of the hotel gurus reveals that while visitors are certainly aware of world events, their immediate concerns have remained job, life style or location specific.

"In light of events in Iraq, we were anticipating our guests to be asking all manner of questions regarding their safety in London and Europe in general, but that hasn't happened," said Richard Price, head concierge at The Royal Garden Hotel in London. Even the notice informing guests that all luggage being left with the bell hops must be searched "hardly raises an eyebrow."

At a New York gathering of hotel executives from far-flung locations such as New Orleans, Italy, Peru and Tahiti, the feeling was largely the same—that safety was not a major concern. One sales manager complained that he knew more about the weather in Iraq than in Chicago, his next destination.

Downtown, at The Regent Wall Street, driving directions to the hotel lead the Top 10 list, followed by limousine reservations to and from airports and a good table for restaurants within the area. Walking directions to Ground Zero was No. 7.

"Of course it depends on the day. You never know what to expect," said Billy DeMelo, chief concierge at XV Beacon Hotel in Boston's historic Beacon Hill area. The boutique hotel near the financial district and Newbury Street shopping caters primarily to business travelers, whose most pressing needs in recent times have been for car service, hard-to-get restaurant reservations and gifts for a spouse.

Location is undeniably a factor in the level of concern.

"It may sound strange, but Shanghai is fairly unaffected by world affairs," said Tina Liu, Grand Hyatt Shanghai communications manager. "We were concerned about what 9/11 would do, but business only increased, and the percentage of Americans as well. I could only guess that when instability hits the U.S. and Europe, the safe place to do business is in China."

Concierge staff in Australia report that the most frequently asked questions are related to life style.

"A request on the rise is for baby sitters, as more guests are traveling with children for either business or pleasure," said Tara Bishop, marketing manager at Grand Hyatt Melbourne.

Guests want to know where to eat and drink, what to see on stage or how to book a winery tour, she said. Location-specific requests include: Where to find kangaroo or crocodile on the menu, where to buy Australian designer clothes and for walking trails around Sydney Harbour.

In the main, it appears to be business as usual.

At one of Japan's top business hotels, Rosewood's Seiyo Ginza in Tokyo, requests vary, but whatever they are "the concierges are still making them happen." When a top American executive wanted T-shirts with his company logo made up in one day, the concierge pulled the logo from the company's homepage and delivered the order.

Resourcefulness is a must, as are connections.

"My latest challenge was a guest who was unable to have a ticket issued on a Brazilian airline that isn't represented here," said John Mark Hopkins at New York's Hotel Plaza Athenee. "I called a travel agent friend in Sao Paulo who not only issued the ticket but sent someone to help her change terminals at the airport. I also made certain she had a mobile phone that worked in Brazil before she left."

Working mobiles and missing rechargers are all part of the job of modern-day concierge staff who are required to be experts on hi-speed Internet connections in guest rooms as well as in hotel conference centers.

And, in some cases, it helps to be clairvoyant.

"'I am coming to New York. What do I do?' is not an unusual question," says Deborah Carr, hotel manager at Le Parker Meridien. "The desk find themselves to be a talking area map. Or, they're asked to be 'Mission Impossible' with last-minute requests for the hottest restaurants or the most difficult theater tickets."

To better assist its guests, the hotel has included a questionnaire on its Web site, http://www.parkermeridien.com. A click on the section title NYC takes them to Explore New York and an additional link "newyorksmartaleck". The answers provide the concierge team with the details necessary to design a customized insider's guide.

A concierge is always prepared to field requests from the routine to the remarkable: from maps and train tables to where to find pretty women and gay bars, how to ship a tuk tuk from Bangkok to America or where to buy a mongoose to deal with snakes in a Vietnam-based guest's backyard.

At the Excelsior Hotel Gallia in Milan, Italy, a concierge is said to have literally saved the life of a tour guide, whose organization was threatening to do away with him because he hadn't been able to find a hot nightclub. The concierge found one.

The staff at Rome's Hotel Eden routinely get questions such as: Is it possible to see the Pope? Can you send postcards from Italy with a U.S. stamp? Or, for a dinner reservation at 6 p.m.—very odd for Italians, who usually dine much later.

Booking tables at top restaurants not only in London, but Paris and the rest of Europe is all in a day's work for The Dorchester's Francis Spiteri, who has also facilitated overseas shipment of one of London's distinctive red telephone booths.

Among the more notable feats of Robert Watson, head concierge at Le Meridien Grosvenor House was to arrange a Baptism in the River Jordan (in Israel), buy gas masks for a family after 9/11, and shipping a crate of English mustard to Dubai.

Donald Birrane, part of the concierge team at the Athenaeum Hotel and Apartments in London also reports there have been no questions regarding security. Among the Top 10, however, are "'What do I do now? What is the windchill factor? And where can I go to eat where there are no Americans?'" The latter question, he hastens to explain, is also asked by Americans, who want the authentic British experience.

(March 2003)

"Reprinted with permission. All rights reserved. © Reuters 2003."

40

Insurance in the Face of Danger

The war is on, and with global travel in a state of flux, the best strategy for business executives seeking peace of mind is to read the fine print on their travel insurance policy.

Though most company employees may be traveling in areas "outside the sphere" of the war in Iraq, a significant number are being sent to the region to provide technical support, one insurance executive said.

"In the current environment, there has been an increase in requests for travel programs to include war risk coverage," said Lloyd Young, senior vice president and chief underwriting officer at American International Companies, members of American International Group, Inc. (AIG), one of a few insurance services providers that does not exclude loss caused by war or terrorism from its coverage.

That does not hold true for a lot of other companies, however.

"The reality is that there are exclusions for war in nearly all travel insurance policies," said Justin McNaull, spokesman in Washington, D.C. for AAA. "If you're in the sphere—the scope of which is subject to interpretation—where the war is going on, travel insurance won't cover you."

As a consequence, more companies are also asking for travel programs to include coverage for terrorism related incidents that might occur in a hotel or other public place, and that can be added to a policy in the form of a rider.

Sales of travel insurance have surged since 9/11 even as the number of business travelers has decreased sharply since the attacks on the United States a year and a half ago.

"Even though there are fewer travelers, a higher percentage of them are buying travel insurance," said Dan McGinnity, a spokesman for Travel Guard International, a travel services provider based in Stevens Point, Wisconsin.

While many Americans curtailed travel plans after September 11, a report from AAA indicates that even more are postponing travel following the start of the Iraq war. Yet even with fewer travelers, the demand for insurance remains the same.

It makes good business sense for companies to show concern for their employees "and would also go a long way to giving travelers peace of mind," said Bob McGovern, employment lawyer at Meyer, Suozzi, English & Klein in New York, who represents individuals as well as employers, from small to mid-size companies.

As the terms and scope of coverage vary, those who find themselves on the road should make it a point to find out exactly what their policy provides—what they are already covered for, and what additional coverage they might need.

Some are automatically covered for accidental death or dismemberment while traveling simply by virtue of paying for their trip with a credit card.

Travel Guard's McGinnity says customers are still most often asking for air-ticket protection plans, which protect travelers who are forced to cancel or change plans. The second-most frequent request is coverage for flight accidents, and the third is collision damage for rental cars.

As frequent travelers continue to face problems such as airlines slashing flights or eliminating routes with little or no notice, trip cancellations are expected to be on the rise.

In response, travel providers are relaxing their policies, by waiving fees and accepting last-minute itinerary changes.

Generally, Americans are taking a "wait-and-see" approach to travel, says Sandra Hughes, vice president of AAA Travel Agency, at the national organization's headquarters in Orlando, Florida.

"We're finding that people are still traveling within their comfort zones," said AAA's McNaull. To help ensure the coverage and flexibility travelers need, he recommends using a travel professional to sift through the jargon and restrictions of the wide array of policies that are available but can be difficult for consumers to understand.

The key is to ask the right questions.

"Talk to the provider to make sure your plan is doing what you think it's doing," McNaull said.

Last week, Travelocity, a pioneer in online travel, teamed with American International Companies to broaden its travel insurance coverage by adding flight protection to its Web site's existing vacation program.

The bottom line, says Travel Guard's McGinnity, is that "in today's travel landscape, any business traveler, whether getting protection through the company or purchasing on their own, should really consider getting travel insurance."

(April 2003)

"Reprinted with permission. All rights reserved. © Reuters 2003."

41

Drawing Up a Corporate Battle Plan

Globe-trotting business executives keeping a close watch on events unfolding over the course of the war in Iraq were left with one clear message: To succeed, you must have a good plan.

The daily military briefings may even have inspired some to come up with their own mission statement to gain the competitive edge in dealing with clients at home or when traveling overseas.

There are strategic similarities to be drawn from the battlegrounds of Iraq and the boardrooms of the corporate world, says U.S. Army war planner and military strategist Lin Todd. He suggests that CEOs might benefit by taking a page from the Army Field Manual.

"If you don't know where you are going in your business, what resources you have at your disposal, or a roadmap on how to get there, you'll never leave your garage—and you'll certainly never compete in today's marketplace, said Todd, whose military expertise has kept him in demand as a radio and television commentator during Operation Iraqi Freedom.

At the U.S. Military Academy at West Point, Todd's courses included Arabic Language and Middle East Studies. In the U.S. Army Staff College, he took part in a program conducted by the School of Advanced Military Studies (SAMS), whose graduates—known as the "Jedi Knights"—wrote Gen. Norman Schwarzkopf's successful, and classic, military plan for Operation Desert Storm in 1991.

"Planning is something the U.S. military does exceedingly well," said Todd. He explained that the battlefield situation, like today's global business environment, tends to change rapidly, and that's where education and training systems come into play.

"When conducting military operations, the U.S. Army follows a cycle that entails planning, preparation, execution, and continuous assessment," he said. "We also make long-term investments in our most critical asset—our people."

"It seems I read every day how this company or that claims that its people are its most important resource," Todd said. "Well, talk is cheap: If you truly believe your people are your most important resource, you'll expend resources to train and educate them. This pays off—period."

The payoff for international meetings planner Joseph Rende, head of Dallas-based Rende Eclectic, comes from his own equation for success: "These People, in This Place, at This Time, for What Purpose."

During 12 years as assistant director of global content creation for the Young Presidents Organization, with members and meetings in 80 countries, Rende followed a strategy of devising "a learning experience" for meeting participants—CEOs of international companies—by showcasing the location of the event, its history and people.

"So often, people do meetings all over the world, but you might as well be at the local airport hotel. The site of the meeting is rarely used to provide context or a backdrop for the content of the meeting," he said.

To create a better understanding, Rende set out to deliver a full sensory experience in every aspect of the meeting—"complete with sound, light and menus."

"When I was doing something in apartheid South Africa, I read everything I could find from all sources on the topic. During research, I came across institutes, think tanks, opinion leaders and celebrities, all of whom become my touchstone for the first on-the-ground meeting."

"I really believe Americans can no longer afford to be 'meeting imperialists.' We need to get out and fully understand how people live around the globe. For the most part, Americans have viewed the world as their own private Disneyland, and now this Disneyland has got consequences that we must fathom and understand and embrace," said Rende. "Meeting planners have a role in shaping, transforming and educating their participants so they are able to walk away with new awareness, deeper understanding and a more profound knowledge of the world around them."

In addition to awareness and understanding, there are still other things considered essential to success in the boardroom—or victory on the battlefield.

And that, says Lin Todd, is where the field manual's doctrinal tenets of Army Operations—Initiative, Agility, Depth, Synchronization and Versatility—come in.

"While those tenets do not guarantee success, their absence risks failure—something which has considerable application in the business world," Todd said.

To illustrate that the faint of heart seldom stand to reap the profits to be gained from new business initiatives, he cited Gen. George S. Patton Jr.'s edict: "A good plan violently executed now is better than a perfect plan next week."

"Agility is a useful quality in today's business leaders, as an ability to successfully parry and thrust against one's competitors can be critical to leading an industry," said Todd. Depth, according to the manual, enables momentum in the offense, elasticity in the defense and staying power in all operations.

The tenet of synchronization—whether it entails prompt delivery of products to minimize inventory costs, or the strategic worldwide coordination of efforts to undermine a competitor's credibility—clearly has applications in business today, he said.

And finally, there's versatility, as demonstrated by the coalition forces in Iraq, who redirected efforts from combat operations to security, humanitarian relief and infrastructure rebuilding projects, Todd said. Companies must also be versatile, whether adapting internally or addressing the needs in today's global marketplace through new outside partnerships.

Any plan, however, is really just a "reasonably accurate forecast of execution," he cautioned, and remains a starting point, not the centerpiece of an operation. "In other words, plan carefully in advance and consider all things, but adjust as necessary to meet the actual challenges."

Arlington, Virginia-based Todd, who has lived and worked in the Middle East, Asia and Europe, is presently involved in a homeland security project to help state and local governments respond to terrorist attacks and other emergencies.

(April 2003)

"Reprinted with permission. All rights reserved. © Reuters 2003."

42

Keeping Their Eyes on the Prize

Budgets remain tight and flight schedules erratic. Security concerns are high and the threat of disease is an added factor. Pent-up frustrations are immense for business travelers, who must stay focused to keep delivering the corporate goods.

"We used to be pampered, now we are searched," said Dr. Terry Paulson, a California-based psychologist and frequent traveler. "The frustration tolerance has been decreased."

With more things beyond their control, travelers need to deal with choices assertively and develop an effective coping style. If they don't, "they are more likely to develop stress-related problems on the road, such as an anger response, or aggressive reaction in the face of frustrations," said Paulson, who has logged 5 million miles as president of the International Federation for Professional Speaking and past president of the National Speakers Association.

Companies are expecting more from traveling staff, and cutting back on trips if the expense cannot be justified. There is increased pressure to perform, and the burden to deliver is also heightened.

"With budget pressures, business travelers are often expected to pick more low-cost travel options, which can mean more flight connections, and all of this increases both their frustration and the challenge, Paulson said.

To help strung-out employees push past obstacles and achieve results, Joyce "The Corporate Coach" Weiss advises companies to "treat the employee like an entrepreneur of his/her own business. Make sure to give them at least 1/2 day off after a long trip, so they will be refreshed when returning to work."

"Keep an open dialogue. Ask in advance about family commitments to make sure there aren't other options that would make the employee happier, such as sharing travel opportunities with a co-worker who may not have children and would be willing and even excited about attending an out-of-town conference or business meeting," said Weiss, an author and founder of Michigan-based Bold Solutions to Boost Their Bottom Line.

Out of town or out of the country, in today's uncertain climate a traveler's reality can change with each destination.

In Casablanca, 12 suicide bombers struck targets as diverse as an Arab-owned five-star hotel, Spanish and Italian restaurants, a Jewish community center, and still more in the vicinity of the Belgian Consulate. Forty-three people, including eight foreigners, were killed.

"What Morocco is doing to reassure business travelers closely mirrors what other civilized countries are doing," said Mohamed Berrada, CEO and chairman of Royal Air Maroc and a former Moroccan minister of finance, who was in New York after attending an airline conference in Washington. "A new anti-terrorism law was passed last week and we have standing agreements with the United States and Europe in the fight against international terrorism."

"There was no reduction in traffic to Morocco following the attacks," said Berrada. "Most of our business travelers come from Europe and they know Morocco better than most Americans. They know that terrorist attacks are international in scope."

In New York, it is often said that another terror attack is not so much a question of "if" but more likely of "when."

But the city is on alert and "as well prepared as anyplace in the world, said Jordan Barowitz, spokesman for Mayor Michael Bloomberg. "We have over 1,000 police officers dedicated solely to counterterrorism."

An added worry is disease. Severe acute respiratory syndrome, or SARS, has spread in Asia as well as to parts of Europe, North and South America.

Indeed with turbulence in all corners of the world, business travel has been pent-up for good reason. But there is a glimmer of light at the end of the tunnel, according to Rosenbluth International corporate travel management services. The Philadelphia-based company's analyst teams are reporting that business travel has moved above pre-war levels, up 20 percent since hitting bottom during the Iraq war and is now just 1 percent under the previous year's levels.

The current activity is "directly related to pent-up demand ... I don't know a CEO or COO on the planet that's not driving growth aggressively," says Ron DiLeo, chief operating officer of Strategic Travel Solutions at RI, which operates in 57 countries.

For most frequent travelers, probably the most complete resource remains the Web site of the U.S. Department of State (http://www.state.gov/travel/), which provides the latest details on SARS, as well as Travel Warnings and Consular information.

(June 2003)

"Reprinted with permission. All rights reserved. © Reuters 2003."

43

Tense Times Put Bosses on Front Lines

As shifting global tensions redraw the boundaries of our comfort zones, the onus is on bosses to reassess risks and motivate workers traveling in areas previously thought to be safe.

In the midst of confusion and rapid change, the key to corporate success is responsible, flexible leadership, security and military experts say.

"When people are scared or uncomfortable, you have to lead. Where you are physically sends an important signal," said Ed Ruggero, a former U.S. Army infantry officer, author and keynote speaker on leader development and ethical leadership.

"Get out there with them—be the first to get on a plane on September 12 or at the conference in Spain," he said, using as examples the Sept. 11, 2001, attacks on New York and Washington and the train bombing in Madrid. "It's the leader's job to reassure people, but you still have to complete the mission."

The success of any mission involves careful preparation.

"Companies need to take a look at insurance policies for people traveling everywhere, not just to typically dangerous areas," said Lin Todd, a military analyst and president of Global Risk, international security consultants based in Arlington, Virginia.

"Most terror attacks are considered acts of war and not covered. Companies have to start budgeting security into contracts and consider insurance for K&R (kidnap and ransom) and medical care as well as provide in-country services, daily briefings and a range of products," Todd said. "It's not cheap, but they will have to start doing it."

Business travelers, even in tense times, need to stay focused and maintain their ability to roll with the punches.

"Successful leaders inspire people and create flexible organizations to get the job done in the face of shifting priorities—even against tremendous odds," says Ruggero, who is preparing a presentation for the CEO European Conference in Palermo, Sicily.

To motivate his clients, which have included Citigroup, Lucent Technologies and SEI Investments, Ruggero draws on combat stories gathered from interviews with war veterans. A graduate of the U.S. Military Academy at West Point, he says his aim at seminars and business conferences is to help develop leaders who are "creative thinkers, who will act when action is called for and who will seek to do the right thing."

Companies also have to take a close look at which air carriers they use and security procedures at airports.

"This is it. It's not going to change," said safety expert Robert L. Siciliano, who believes that travelers' concerns have neither increased nor decreased in light of recent events.

"Post 9/11, corporations and individual business travelers have a heightened awareness regarding personal safety. The tragedy in Spain has only reaffirmed beliefs that terrorism is going to continue," said Siciliano, who has 18 years of experience in self-defense, security work and martial arts.

In his book "The Safety Minute," Boston-based Siciliano explains verbal and physical self-defense techniques, lethal and non-lethal products in personal protection as well as the emotions experienced during an attack. At his Web sites http://www.SafeTravelSecurity.com and http://www.SafetyMinute.com, he addresses problems such as political unrest and assaults against business travelers.

"If anything, security will become tighter. Sooner rather than later, all Americans will be identified through the use of biometrics ... iris scan, voice recognition or thumbprint," Siciliano said. "You'll see corporate travel managers being diligent about educating sales staff and employees."

Meanwhile, he says travelers should abide by federal Transportation Security Administration (TSA) guidelines, which are constantly changing. "Whether they are reasonable or perceived as unreasonable, it is not for us to judge."

Another source for updates on potential terror threats and protective measures is the "Homeland Security and Traveler Information" link at The American Hotel & Lodging Association (AH&LA) Web site, http://www.ahla.com.

As travel plans continue to be overcome by events, priorities will change. But management must remain optimistic and calm, said Ed Ruggero, quoting World War II commanding General and U.S. President Dwight D. Eisenhower: "Any anxieties I feel, I save for my pillow at night."

"Anxiety is overpowering, and it helps if you put things into perspective," Ruggero said. "If a staffer is having a meltdown the day before a trip, it may have to be postponed. The company must evaluate the risks and help people articulate their fears. Everyone has a breaking point, but it is not a moral failure—it is something that you deal with."

But harsh realities cannot be ignored. The worst could happen, so it is best to be as prepared as possible with forms of whom to notify in case of an accident.

"Military people put their lives on the line; business people not as often," he said. "But that line is getting blurred."

(March 2004)

"Reprinted with permission. All rights reserved. © Reuters 2004."

44

Survival of the Fittest

Don't travel alone. Steer clear of crowds. Remain inconspicuous. Keep in touch. Locate hotel room air vents. Report suspicious activity. Know which way the wind blows. Carry a handkerchief and gloves. Business travelers need to know a lot to survive in today's world.

Iraq, economic instability and homeland security continue to dominate headlines: New York to use 15,000-pound metal barriers to guard political convention site; Business magazine editor murdered in Moscow; London Heathrow airport anti-terror documents found at the roadside.

"Always anticipate the unexpected," says former New York City Police Commissioner Howard Safir. "Our adversaries are innovative and well trained. We need to be alert to all possibilities, and avoid taking unnecessary risks.

"If traveling in a country where there is anti-American feeling, go about your business but be as inconspicuous as possible," said Safir, chairman and CEO of New York-based SafirRosetti security consulting, investigative and intelligence firm (http://www.safirrosetti.com) with offices in seven U.S. cities, London and Hong Kong. "We teach people how to take evasive action, depending on what they're confronted with."

Americans—perceived as being rich and guaranteeing headlines—are targets of many organizations, and in areas such as Asia or the Middle East, they stand out, said Dan Braccia, founder and managing partner of Crisis Team Training, (http://www.crisisteamtraining.com) based in Orange County, New York. With 15 years of law enforcement experience, Braccia, a former NYPD Academy instructor, took early retirement to join the federal air marshall program after Sept. 11, 2001.

"Corporate travelers must be proactive," said Braccia, who has written The Emergency Preparedness Handbook, a step-by-step process for dealing with a crisis, and hosts a talk radio show on crisis management for Clear Channel.

"Find out your company's current emergency management plan. When was it last updated? What if you are injured and lying in a hospital. Where does the bill go? Confirm there's a plan in place to get you back home," Braccia said.

"Give your spouse a detailed itinerary and phone regularly. Create sources of contact who will be concerned if they don't hear from you and put the wheels in motion to provide direction on your whereabouts," he said.

Braccia recommends staying in a brand-name hotel—an American chain. In a country where a threat exists, he says, their management will be more U.S.-friendly and have a plan as well as a solid connection back home.

"Try to get a room on the second or third floors. In case of fire, first responders can still get to you. Stay away from ground floors, in case of demonstrations or attacks," says environmental counterterrorism expert Elsa Lee, with more than 20 years of experience in anti-terrorism, counterespionage, threat and vulnerability assessments in the United States, Asia, Central America and Europe.

In a high-rise building, "make sure someone knows how to shut off the HVAC (heating, ventilation and air conditioning) system in case of suspicious vapors, mist or smoke," said Lee, CEO of Advantage SCI (http://www.advantagesci.com) based in Redondo Beach, California.

In case of a bioterror attack, you will see dead animals or people getting sick, she said. "Make your direction of escape against the wind. Use any clothing available to cover your mouth and filter your breathing. Get in the habit of carrying a clean handkerchief and plastic gloves."

Listen to your instincts, and always be on the lookout for things out of the ordinary.

"Look for someone leaving a briefcase or a package. Or people dressed inappropriately for the weather—wearing an overcoat on a 90-degree (32 C) day," said Safir. "Report it and remove yourself from the area."

Do not take things into your own hands.

"I strongly urge people not to interfere. Make a visual picture of the suspicious activity. Do not be afraid to pick up the phone. The worst thing that can happen is that you're wrong. So what? Think of the alternative," Braccia said.

A business traveler's mode of local transportation—whether bus, taxi or rental car—should be dictated by the country. In Israel, for example, it's best to avoid public transport, which is commonly targeted by suicide bombers.

If driving, "veer away from street jams and crowds whenever possible," advises Lee. "Abandon the car if necessary."

"Get clear directions. Jessica Lynch got lost and drove into an ambush," said Braccia, referring to an incident involving a U.S. Army supply convoy that took a wrong turn in Iraq. "If getting from Point A to Point B involves driving through an unstable area, find out how to get around it."

(July 2004)

"Reprinted with permission. All rights reserved. © Reuters 2004."

Part VIII
Travel Trends

POLITICAL GLOBE
GULF OF MEXICO
MEXICO
GUATEMALA
EL SALVADOR
COSTA RICA
PANAMA
ECUADOR
GALAPAGOS ISLANDS
PERU
LEGEND

45

Charity begins at work

By taking part in pleasurable activities like a bicycle race, wine tasting or celebrity cocktail party, business travelers can help feed the hungry, combat AIDS, diabetes or MS, and educate and motivate youth.

Hotel stays that coincide with special events, where proceeds benefit charities such as cancer research, education and other good causes, can also be emotionally profitable.

"Helping others can expand the healthy part of your personality," says Dr. Jason Kornrich, a psychologist.

"While enjoying a nice hotel room, some might feel a little guilty, and being instrumental in helping to transfer funds or resources to a charity could relieve some of that guilt," said Kornrich, the director of Ambulatory Mental Health Services at Nassau University Medical Center, in East Meadow, New York.

Popular charitable causes are youth projects and fighting life-threatening disease, while favored means include auctions, sports activities and food or beverage related events.

The inspiration for Isadore Sharpe, founder of the Four Seasons hotel chain, to organize annual fundraising events at his hotels around the world came from Terry Fox, a young Canadian who lost his battle with bone cancer at age 22 in 1981. The Terry Fox Run, hosted by the Four Seasons Hotel in Washington one year brought in $60,000 for the Washington Cancer Institute.

"Creativity is key when it comes to cancer fundraising efforts at Four Seasons Resort Palm Beach ... from 5K Runs to employee-sponsored car washes," said Harry Gorstayn, general manager of the Florida hotel. "This year, we're hosting our first charity golf tournament and also having a wine auction. Every year, we raise about $10,000 to fund ongoing research."

In the fight against MS, about $35,000 is raised annually by the Reno/Tahoe Winter Wine & Ski Expo in Nevada at The Atlantic Casino Resort in conjunction with the Huega Foundation for Multiple Sclerosis. Forty wineries, five microbreweries, 20 restaurants and 12 ski resorts recently took part.

Top donors mingle with movie legends and rock stars in the St. Regis Monarch Beach Resort & Spa at a benefit for the AIDS Services Foundation of Orange County, California. One gala was attended by Elizabeth Taylor, Warren Beatty and Tom Petty, whose guitar was auctioned for $9,000.

The 12th Annual Hare Racing Experience to benefit the Epilepsy Services Foundation was hosted in the spring by The Doubletree Guest Suites Tampa Bay in Florida, where the 5K, 10K and 1-mile walk/run netted $9,000.

Many efforts put emphasis on community involvement.

"It's the right thing to do," Jan Larsen, general manager of the Millenium Hilton in New York's financial district. "We have adopted the Millenium High School in lower Manhattan as our annual charitable fund-raising activity." Their efforts translate into special study programs, educational and extracurricular activities and career days.

In the Washington D.C. community, members of Congress, business moguls and celebrities come together for The Madison Battle of the Hill at Renditions Golf Club in Davidsonville, Maryland. Hosted by The Madison hotel, the inaugural tournament raises funds for The First Tee of Washington, to promote positive values for underprivileged youth.

A good time to appeal to people's generosity is during holidays.

The Saturday after Thanksgiving, The Broadmoor in Colorado Springs, Colorado, hosts a "White Lights Ceremony" with the American Cancer Society. As part of "Love Lights a Tree," community members can purchase a light in memory or honor of cancer victims or survivors.

The Gingerbread Village is created annually in The Sheraton Seattle Hotel & Towers lobby from late November until after Christmas by local architects and the hotel's pastry chefs. The event draws more than 100,000 viewers, whose donations over 11 years have raised $175,000 for the Juvenile Diabetes Research Foundation.

Other worthwhile causes include senior citizens, nature conservancy, love of country and preservation of culture.

Since its inception in 1999, Embassy Suites Portland Downtown's Dineout Reception has raised more than half a million dollars for Meals-on-Wheels, which delivers about 4,000 hot meals every weekday to homebound seniors in Portland, Oregon.

In Natural Bridge, Virginia, the Inn & Conference Center co-sponsors Celebrate Liberty Weekend to honor the U.S. armed forces. The beneficiary, Toy

Museum at Natural Bridge, run by the Society for the Preservation of American Childhood Effects, displays artifacts dating from 1740.

Would-be do-gooders are advised, however, to apply due diligence before committing funds, says Daniel Borochoff, president of the American Institute of Philanthropy in Chicago. "It is important to separate the charity from actual benefits received. It's like writing two checks—one for the food and entertainment participants receive and the other for charity. Only the portions going to the charity could be tax deductible."

(October 2003)

"Reprinted with permission. All rights reserved. © Reuters 2003."

46

A Woman's Changing World

By 2005, women are expected to exceed 50 percent of the total number of business travelers. With distinct preferences, practical needs and significant purchasing power, they are making the travel industry sit up and take notice.

The average woman business traveler, according to statistics from a variety of industry sources, is over 40, married with no children, has a management job, and, with an income of about $68,000, is often the primary or sole wage earner. She spends $175 billion on 14 million trips a year.

Yet despite her growing presence in the global corporate arena, a woman traveling solo can be vulnerable to theft or physical attack, making on-the-road security a top concern.

"Exposure to hostile environments can occur in any community, at work, or while traveling on company business," says Darlene Radloff, director of security training for Air Security International in Houston, Texas.

Radloff—with 27 years of experience in the aviation industry including airport and ground operations security—has designed a one-day course "For Women Only—Safety & Security Training" that teaches preventive techniques and offers safety tips for hotel rooms, elevators, parking lots, rental cars and how to survive a kidnapping.

After personal safety, another important consideration for traveling female executives is the proximity to clients.

"I try to stay in the vicinity of one of our restaurants," said Washington, D.C.-based Ellen Robinson, who logged 135,000 miles last year as director of catering sales for Palm Management Corp., with 28 properties in the United States, Puerto Rico and Mexico.

"In a lot of cities where cabs are not readily available, I have the name of a reputable car service so I don't have to worry about being overcharged or ending up in the wrong part of town," she said in a phone interview from Troy, Michigan.

"One week I was in Los Angeles, Atlanta and Washington, and the week before in Tampa, Charlotte and Nashville," said Robinson, who has already flown 40,000 miles this year.

Women who do business internationally often deal with two major pitfalls of nonverbal communication: power and sex.

"What women take for granted as normal confidence can be seen as arrogant or manly in some parts of the world. The signals we use to communicate warmth and openness can be seen as hot and far too open," said Patti Wood, an Atlanta-based behavior expert, trainer and international speaker. "This can cause problems."

"When doing business in Germany, men will stand when a woman enters a room and if they are talking to you they will remain standing till you sit down," she said. "Don't make a funny comment or say please sit down. Germans would find the humor rude and aggressive coming from a woman."

Misreading the signals while negotiating with foreign counterparts can also create problems.

"Germans don't smile during business," said Wood, known as The Body Language Lady, "and a standard warm smile could be misinterpreted as a come-on."

"In France, it is common to have strong extended eye contact during business interactions. If a Frenchman gives you extended eye contact in a business interaction, don't misinterpret it and think, 'He wants me!'" Wood warned.

However, the same extended eye contact from a businessman in a country with a strong machismo culture could very well mean "he wants you," she said.

What women travelers want most when it comes to accommodations is responsive service (90 percent), location (71) and affordable rates (62 percent), a Wyndham Hotels & Resorts survey found.

The "Woman Aware Campaign" in Britain promotes safety for female travelers. Among the Top 10 criteria it uses to rate hotels are "a well-lit, secure parking lot or valet parking, room security locks, permanently lit corridors, peepholes and discreet room number allocation," says Kelvin Houchin, executive vice president of Radisson Edwardian hotels in London.

Another example is Lady's First, a 28-room boutique hotel for women only, in Zurich, Switzerland. Designed by a woman architect and with an all-female staff, it provides an atmosphere for guests to congregate in comfort, avoiding the awkward experience that can occur in a hotel bar or restaurant, where a woman alone might call unwanted attention to herself.

Sofitel luxury hotels appeal to female travelers with "nine points of distinction" such as a prestigious address, uniforms by Parisian designer Jean-Charles de Castelbajac, Roger & Gallet amenities and restaurants with high-profile chefs.

The hotel industry recognizes that anticipating the needs of women travelers is good business.

(May 2003)

"Reprinted with permission. All rights reserved. © Reuters 2003."

47

An Alternative Point of View

Gays are discerning business travelers who tend to take more work-related trips than their non-gay counterparts, an online study reveals.

When choosing a hotel, they list cost, location and fair treatment as the most important factors, according to a consumer research study conducted by Witeck-Combs Communications and Harris Interactive.

"These findings are not surprising," says Wesley Combs, president of Witeck-Combs, which consults with major U.S. corporations marketing to GLBT (gay, lesbian, bisexual and transgender) consumers. "Because only 20 percent of GLB households have children, it may be that GLB employees have fewer conflicts when it comes to business travel. Given this assumption, they may more readily volunteer, or might possibly be asked to take more business trips."

John Madden, a Florida-based bank officer whose work takes him to Latin America and the Caribbean about once a month, said gay business travelers basically fit into two main categories—individuals who work for corporate America and those who are self-employed or in creative, less mainstream occupations.

Their job category also may dictate their choice of lodgings, where the cutting-edge minimalist touch generally holds more appeal for gay travelers.

"I work in a traditional corporate setting and have no choice," Madden said. "My corporate travel agency books accommodations. If I had my own business, I may decide to stay at a guesthouse or other establishment.

"But, while I do work for a traditional company, I am not working 24 hours a day," he said. "I might want to go out after work and see what the nightlife is like."

That is where it's important to do some research on your destination and be aware of different laws.

"If you're checking out the nightlife, you need to make sure that type of lifestyle is accepted within the country. For instance, don't go to Paraguay expecting to have a major party. In Rio, it's very different and very open," he said.

"Depending on where you travel in Europe, Latin America or the United States, gay bookstores sell guidebooks on what to do, where not to go, and names of hotels and restaurants."

Big cities tend to be more tolerant. They recognize that supporting the gay community, a segment that nationwide spends more than $54 billion a year on travel, is a smart economic move. Within that community is also a powerful network for executives.

"When it comes to corporate America, everyone has gotten more gay friendly," said J. Travis, media director for the Kimberly, a boutique hotel in midtown Manhattan.

"Gay corporate America appreciates individuality and is looking for a unique experience, which is understood, especially in a city like New York. When you are away on business you appreciate that even more," Travis said. "One of the things that appeals about the Kimberly is that it is a higher-end product, but with a value. We are an all-suite hotel so guests have an office and a place to entertain with a full kitchen so they are not limited to restaurants if they are on a budget."

Andrea Sertoli, president of Select Italy (www.selectitaly.com)—a custom-travel company with offices in Chicago, Rome and Florence—said their findings reveal that "the minimalist touch tends to be more appealing to the gay traveling community, whereas other travelers may be more inclined to stay in classic or Baroque-style hotels."

"The whole topic is elusive—from the perspective of designers to the general appeal to gay aesthetic sensibilities," said Neil Goodman, research and production manager at Select Italy, who spent several years in Rome. "(Gays) find the so-called boutique hotels particularly welcome. These hotels are popping up all over the place, each more stylish than the next—all cutting edge, with very sophisticated, very modern design.

"Our clientele is mixed-gay/straight, business/leisure, but we are looking forward to offering gay-oriented tours of Italy," he said.

In London, the gay scene is as diverse and progressive as its gay population, according to Chris Lynn, New York-based sales and marketing director representing business and conventions for Visit London in the North American market. "Marketing for people traveling to London in some respects is quite generic. Whether leisure or business, we find that many are maximizing their time by combining the two."

In an effort to "support decision making" for gay visitors, The London Tourist Board launched the 100-page Gay & Lesbian London Guide, (http://

www.visitlondon.com/gay) with tips on dining out, insider shopping, spas, gyms, clubs and more.

And, Philadelphia has begun a marketing campaign for gay and lesbian travelers. (http://www.gophila.com.)

In today's competitive market, the Witeck-Combs survey said, "It is increasingly important for hotels to create a welcoming and respectful environment for all guests, including GLB customers."

(August 2003)

"Reprinted with permission. All rights reserved. © Reuters 2003."

48

The Expatriate Life

The prospect of an overseas assignment may have many corporate executives walking on air. But the logistics of setting up a household halfway round the world, will bring them down to earth in a flash.

Expatriates, even while caught up in the excitement and the prospect of advancement, must at the same time be able to perform well on the job, manage cultural differences, find schools for the children and keep a spouse happy.

As U.S. companies continue rapid expansion overseas, they must choose candidates wisely.

"In today's global organizations, having an international viewpoint and business experience may be a prerequisite for an executive-level position," said Sherry Harsch-Porter, founder of The Porter Bay Groups, an international consulting company based in St. Louis. "International assignments give employees a keen edge for future promotions."

But people with international experience are not in great supply, making it an expensive gamble for both sides.

"The cost of sending a mid-level manager on a three-year international assignment can easily exceed $1 million," Harsch-Porter said. Consequently, to have assignments fail or a repatriated manager leave the company is a disaster.

In searching for the right candidate, companies look for certain profiles. The top three most desirable traits for an international candidate and spouse are maturity/emotional stability, introspection and intelligence.

To head off low productivity, expats are encouraged to communicate any fears or uncertainties during the adjustment period. Some companies provide a hotline for their employees and families to call if they encounter even routine problems, such as setting up a bank account or dealing with a neighbor.

"Expectations vary a great deal from culture to culture and difficulty can arise between bosses and subordinates," said Sheida Hodge, Worldwide Managing

Director of the Cross-Cultural Division for Berlitz International Inc., which provides training for orientation and relocation.

"Global savvy is required for success," she said, citing a complex example of one client—a German from Spain working in France for an American boss.

"France and Spain are very hierarchical and there is a lot of respect for managers. Do not call them by their first names and do not contradict them—openly or privately," she said.

"In Austria and Germany, authority is based on expertise. So, if the boss is not an expert on a certain topic, the subordinate has a right to challenge him," said Hodge Berlitz, with 450 locations in more than 60 countries worldwide, offers a two-day program for expats-to-be.

"The purpose is to give them an understanding for what is awaiting them," Hodge said. "Day One deals with the nuts and bolts of living in a country and Day Two is about business culture and managing one's career in a new environment."

Adequate preparation is significant, because the most common reason that overseas assignments fail is the inability of the employee's family to adapt.

"Employees offered an international assignment must often choose between what is best for their career and what's best for their family," Harsch-Porter said. "This is particularly true when trailing spouses have to derail their own careers."

Generally, the greater the cultural difference, the greater the difficulty in adjusting.

Yet, from a U.S. perspective, anecdotal evidence indicates the assignment most likely to fail is in Britain.

"When Americans go to Britain, they think it will be just like here. But, even with a common language, they go through a profound culture shock because the way business is done is very different, often resulting in failed expectations on both sides," said Harsch-Porter. "The company doesn't prepare employees well enough and they, in turn, expect things to be different than they are."

Conversely, says Berlitz' Hodge, foreigners get confused when they come here, expecting open and friendly relations.

"U.S. companies are much more hierarchical than traditional, but it's not a power thing. Americans value efficiency and timeliness," Hodge said. "Managers get paid a lot to make quick decisions and foreigners may get completely disoriented. Americans, on the other hand, need to be more patient and slow-paced if going to work in Japan."

While recent surveys show that companies have been more hesitant to relocate employees overseas, Harsch-Porter said, the reason is not, as some believe, due to safety issues brought about by the attacks of Sept. 11, 2001.

"It seems to be more a reflection of the economy," she said. "And, as a greater percentage of revenue is generated outside the headquarters country, finding leaders with international expertise is likely to remain a priority."

(January 2004)

"Reprinted with permission. All rights reserved. © Reuters 2004."

49

Middle East Meets West

Political agendas, culture gaps and excessive travel curbs present the biggest challenges to doing business in the global marketplace today, according to a group of influential Arab and Western businesswomen.

Those factors combine to curtail mobility, which is critical to managing change in the global economy, the panel of executives representing France, Lebanon, Saudi Arabia, United Arab Emirates, United Kingdom and the United States agreed at the Wf360 Arab-Western Businesswomen's Summit.

"The world is multi-ethnic. Today, the organization is not in one place—it fits everywhere," said Sheikha Lubna Al Qasimi, Chief Executive of Tejari, the Middle East's premier electronic business-to-business marketplace.

The panel urged companies to encourage travel and find ways for their people to travel freely across borders to preserve the stability globalized business operations can create.

"Organizations as well as governments need to put in the effort, or the business side will suffer," said Qasimi at the Wf360 summit in New York. "The perception and image of the U.S. is that of distrust. In our organization, visas have been denied for security reasons."

For global business to thrive, there has to be a climate of ease, security and trust, says Thuraya al Arrayed, consultant, Saudi Arabian Affairs, Saudi Aramco petroleum company, which has the world's largest oil reserves.

"The pollution of the business environment with political agenda manipulations of business requirements and procedures ... makes it difficult to do business as usual," said Arrayed, who suggests that a "positive change" in U.S. Middle East foreign policy would "calm inflamed feelings."

After Sept. 11, 2001, Americans severely cut back on travel abroad. A more recent development, said Nayla Rene Moawad, a member of Parliament in Lebanon, is that fewer people are traveling both ways.

"Traveling to the U.S. is perceived as more problematic. But networking is important," said Moawad, an advocate for human rights, fair government and economic independence for women.

Business leaders must learn to think globally, act locally, understand the difference and apply their knowledge.

Lubna Al Olayan, CEO of Olayan Financing Company in Saudi Arabia, said more emphasis should be put on local partners.

"We must be aggressive about hiring and training local leaders as your eyes and ears," Diane Gulyas, group Vice president, DuPont Electronic & Communication Technologies, agreed. "Give them skills ... then trust and listen to them."

Chicago-based president of Alcoa Closure Systems International, Sandra Beach Lin, who has lived and worked in Singapore, also advocates spending time with local customers and suppliers. "Alcoa is in 300 locations, but tastes for Coca-Cola are different. You must capture the differences," she said.

Arrayed said there needs to be a common link. "It should be mutually beneficial for a win-win situation. But, be attuned to feelings. Give them what they can accept, not just what you think they want or need."

That is where a good local manager becomes invaluable—to point out mistakes and explain how to rectify them.

"How you do something is just as important as what you do ... we are human as well," said London-based Helen Alexander, chief executive of The Economist Group, publisher of The Economist newspaper and Economist.com. She said her major challenge is "understanding customers—how they think, how they change."

To bridge cultural gaps, the panel recommended reaching out to future customers and future business leaders.

"Younger people are more familiar with brands and are better consumers," said Lebanon's Moawad.

"You have to start early. I would encourage young people to travel," said Christine Lagarde, chairman, Global Executive Committee, Baker & McKenzie in Paris, one of the world's largest law firms, with a staff of over 8,000 in 66 countries. A drawback to business travel today, she said, is "lack of predictability—much longer delays, endless queuing, physical searches ... and general suspicion when crossing the U.S. border."

Strict security is understandable, but at some point it becomes counterproductive.

"I've never seen anti-American feeling as high as today—even in Asia where you wouldn't expect it ... Politics is becoming a business issue," said Gulyas.

Corporate ethics are also a concern around the world, although globalization is slowly imposing a value system.

"In Southeast Asia, the solution to corruption is to appoint female judges," said Lagarde, whose specialty is antitrust and labor law. "They already have an income (from husbands) and are perceived as less susceptible (to bribes).

"Clearly, a set of common principles is needed. Honesty is fundamental and universal. We must adjust locally. The rules are there—but not always enforced."

(April 2004)

"Reprinted with permission. All rights reserved. © Reuters 2004."

50

Making a World of Difference.

Working in poverty-stricken areas gives corporate travelers an up-close look at global problems such as disease, illiteracy or injustice. It also puts them in a position to bring about change.

It can be as simple as sharing knowledge, volunteering time, donating possessions or enlisting the aid of friends, colleagues and employers.

"When executives are in disadvantaged areas, the first instinct is to do something immediately ... and reach into their pockets for money," said Lelei LeLaulu, president and chief executive of Counterpart International (http://www.counterpart.org), which helps develop small businesses in emerging economies around the world. "But that is not usually the most effective way."

What's needed is a longer-term approach that yields greater rewards.

"Large corporations get the best possible rates. By offering their purchasing leverage to a non-profit agency to get equipment they need, they can leverage $30,000 into over $1 million in medicine and medical equipment," said LeLaulu, whose organization also trains at-risk youth in information technology and provides humanitarian assistance in countries such as Iraq, Ghana, Haiti and Moldova.

Being there creates the critical connection.

"Global travel can make it possible for people themselves to be the living link to world resources," says Nancy Rivard, president of Airline Ambassadors International.

"Travel has given me a much broader appreciation of our common humanity," said Rivard, whose 5,000 AAI members have hand-delivered more than $14 million worth of aid to orphanages, clinics and remote communities in 44 countries. "There is a personal awareness of the physical inequity that exists when it comes to medicine, clean water, education ... even a comfortable place to sleep."

An employee of American Airlines since 1976, Rivard has used her flight privileges and free time to travel around the world. A longing for greater meaning in life led her to establish AAI and form ties with the United Nations and the U.S. Congress. Her earlier efforts included rallying colleagues to collect hotel amenities for widows in Bosnia and escorting children in need of medical assistance.

She has since been honored as 1999 Woman of Peace, 2000 Ambassador of Peace, with the 2003 National Caring Award and 2004 President's Award for Lifetime Achievement.

"People—be they doctors, scientists or celebrities—want to make a difference, but one of the problems is that they don't know how," said Sylvia Dostal, administrative director for California-based AAI.

Chilean-born Dostal, who owned an interior design business for 25 years, is using her organizational skills "to create an infrastructure for us to be successful. We identify skills that are necessary and partner with other organizations," she said.

Missions are varied. One AAI team took 2,000 pairs of new shoes to a refugee camp near San Salvador. Teams currently are digging wells, planting gardens and building a clinic. Upcoming opportunities to help are listed on AAI's Web site (http://www.airlineamb.org) and include locations such as Argentina, Ecuador, India, Cambodia and Serbia.

On AAI's wish list are things such as gently used baseball gloves, bats and balls, first-aid items, laptop computers, jeans and sweaters.

"I see a change in underlying values," said Rivard, who continues to work as a flight attendant and does one humanitarian mission a month.

Virgin Atlantic supports charities worldwide by collecting envelopes of loose coins from its passengers. It responded to the humanitarian crisis in Sudan by dedicating its onboard Change for Children to the Disasters Emergency Committee's Sudan Emergency Appeal.

The British-based airline also took up a collection for the American Red Cross Disaster Fund to help those affected by the Sept. 11, 2001, terror attacks in New York, Washington D.C. and Pennsylvania.

Counterpart International—whose leadership includes prominent names like Mark Silverstein of The Skin Cancer Foundation, Eamon M. Kelly of the National Science Foundation, Gail Moaney of Ruder Finn and founding patron Sophia Loren—is changing the way private companies are operating in developing countries, said LeLaulu. "Non-profits need to speak to the corporate world to mix creativities. We can do a lot together.

"Our local workers are good, but they need to learn the finer points. If we could get a professional accountant or bookkeeper to train my bookkeepers in Africa or Central Asia for two weeks, it would make an enormous difference," he said. "It would be a life-changing experience. These are the sorts of things traveling executives should be thinking about."

(August 2004)

"Reprinted with permission. All rights reserved. © Reuters 2004."

51

Meeting of Minds on the Seas

Taking the waters has long been the recommended way to relieve stress. So it's not surprising that, after a year of tension and losses, business leaders planning corporate retreats are trading their frequent flyer wings for water wings.

Cruise companies say incentive bookings are on the rise since September 11. As businesses put a priority on rewarding employees for a job well done, cost-effective shipboard getaways can also make it easier to stay within budget guidelines.

With New York also experiencing a rebirth as a passenger ship port, business-at-sea specialist Landry & Kling Inc., the Florida-based company that pioneered the concept of corporate cruises in 1982, says the industry is ready.

"Cruise lines are continuing to build new vessels and most ships are sailing at full capacity. They are also showing profits," said Richelle Taylor marketing manager at Landry & Kling. "We have found that our corporate group bookings have returned to pre-9/11 levels."

"The trend post 9/11 is also to cost-cutting," Richard Weinstein, vice president of corporate and incentive sales for the world's largest cruise line, Miami-based Carnival Corp. said.

The price of a cruise already includes the room, food and beverage, entertainment, activities and fitness club facilities.

"Incentive groups are coming back big-time," said Eric Graves, vice president of group sales for Los Angeles-based Crystal Cruises. "They went into their shell for eight months, but interestingly in the last 30 to 60 days, there started to be an optimism. Insurance companies, automobile dealerships, recreational vehicle companies all want to reward their sales people." And, professionals no longer have to worry about "disappearing" on the ocean.

"What's also helping cruise ships is that busy business people—lawyers, doctors—are thrilled that technically advanced capabilities aboard a ship are just as good as on land. That has truly changed the complexion of why groups are ready to go on ships," said Graves, adding that Crystal is very excited about going into New York.

The time factor is also key for corporate groups.

"When scheduling meetings, people are looking for a short time frame. We have three-day cruises from Florida, Texas or Southern California, where ships present the opportunity for companies looking to conduct meetings," Carnival's Weinstein said.

He believes a ship also presents a "huge" bonding advantage over a land-based venue.

"Another benefit of conducting a meeting on a ship is that there's a camaraderie that doesn't exist in a hotel—or only to a limited degree when people meet up in a bar afterward. On a ship, all the activity takes place within a contained environment. You have a huge opportunity for colleague bonding—to have meals together, see shows, spend off-time together," Weinstein said. "That seems to be the sort of thing people are now putting an emphasis on in all facets of life."

Of the more than 185 departures scheduled from the Port of New York, a record number of 52 sailings are planned by Carnival Corp., which owns Holland America, Cunard, Seabourn, Costa, and Windstar cruises. Among them are a weeklong cruise from New York to Bermuda, four and five-day Canada voyages and several two and three-day sailings.

The marketing group for Radisson Seven Seas cruise ships also reports an increase in ships being used for incentive trips. RSSC, part of Minneapolis-based Carlson Companies Inc., has scheduled 14 New York departures to Bermuda and Canada and New England from May through October next year.

Landry & Kling's Taylor said it is important to note that cruise lines have taken additional measures to further enforce security since 9/11.

"A ship is a safe controlled environment for a meeting, incentive or conference. A ship also offers financial security on your corporate investment because of the ability to move out of a sensitive geographic location when necessary," she said.

The Cruise Line International Association (CLIA), which represents 23 North American cruise lines and 17,000 travel agencies, reports that the industry as a whole has rebounded dramatically since last September, with a 3.8 percent increase in the number of cruisers in the first half of 2002, compared with the same period in 2001 and is on track to meet its target of a record 7.4 million North American passengers in 2002.

The cruise industry contributed almost $18 billion to the U.S. economy and generated more than 257,000 jobs in 2000, according to the Washington-based

Ocean Conservancy, a nonprofit organization dedicated to protecting ocean environments.

To learn more about types of business cruises, choosing the right ship, meeting facilities, cost comparisons and tax deductibility, visit http://www.landrykling.com. The site also offers information on planning conventions, sales meetings, customer appreciation, seminars at sea, golf at sea and full-ship charters as well as a free video including testimonials from planners who have arranged meetings for companies such as computer services firm Electronic Data Systems Corp (EDS), General Casualty Insurance Companies and electronics retailer RadioShack.

Details are also available from the Web sites for individual cruise lines, such as http://www.Carnival.com, Radisson Seven Seas Cruises (http://www.rssc.com) and http://www.CrystalCruises.com.

(September 2003)

"Reprinted with permission. All rights reserved. © Reuters 2003."

52

Onward and Upward

In the waning weeks of 2004, a positive note: Two of the travel industry's hardest-hit segments—domestic business travel and international inbound travel—will see their first increases since before Sept. 11, 2001.

Americans will take 144 million business trips by the end of this year, 4 percent more than in 2003, the Travel Industry Association of America annual survey says.

As new venues open in Europe, Asia and the Middle East, experts in corporate leadership, worldwide development and international law agree that opportunities are rife for U.S. companies to generate business, goodwill and optimism.

"Business travel in Asia has really come back, with so much going on in China that cuts costs," said Jack O'Neill, executive vice president and chief operating officer in the United States for Carlson Wagonlit Travel. "Major airlines see their expansion lying overseas. There is a battle for more Beijing service."

Experienced travelers continue to strive to be more efficient "by embracing new security processing such as pupil scan, using self-check kiosks, and printing boarding passes online the night before a trip," he said.

Developments in Iraq and changes in U.S. policy lifting trade sanctions in Libya will bring "business travel that hasn't been happening in the past," said Curt Dombek, international trade expert and partner at Bryan Cave LLP in Los Angeles. Though Syria sanctions have been tightened, he said Libya offers opportunities in oil and gas as well as technology, telecoms and computers.

"A range of business equipment is needed for an economy that is now expected to develop more significantly," said Dombek.

Libya is still subject to anti-terrorism controls, however, and therefore not in the same general category as other developing countries, he cautioned.

"There's a fair amount of unease, a shift in attitudes in the Arab world post the Iraq invasion," said Dombek, who represented the Kuwait government after the

Gulf War and advises clients on international regulatory issues, including export controls, customs and corruption.

"It remains to be seen how welcome U.S. companies will be," he said. "Kuwait is receptive, but the environment has changed. Trends and economic sanctions are impossible to predict."

Meanwhile, social responsibility and ethical leadership can help build bridges.

"Much of the outside world perceives the United States with a combination of hostility, resignation and curiosity," said Lelei LeLaulu, president and CEO of Washington-based Counterpart International (http://www.counterpart.org). "It is a great opportunity to reach out a hand in friendship.

"There has been a tendency to just grow and not look too closely at host communities," he said. "The business sector might consider taking an extra step or two toward their local stakeholders."

LeLaulu suggests that U.S. airlines follow the lead of Air Jamaica, which holds town hall meetings in New York, Philadelphia, Washington and Boston.

"Discussions cover immigration, financial freedom and real estate. The result? Community support, a strong customer base and brand loyalty."

Today's problems might be more easily managed if CEOs looked to the past for guidance and positive inspiration, says West Point graduate Ed Ruggero, a former infantry officer, teacher and the author of nine books.

Ruggero, a corporate speaker on ethical leadership (http://www.edruggero.com), applies the lessons of history, retelling personal accounts of courage, motivation and leadership in difficult circumstances.

In a dramatic illustration, he took U.S. business executives on a tour of the Normandy battlefield in France shortly before the 60th anniversary of D-Day, June 6, 1944.

The CEO of the company, which had experienced a rough patch, wanted to make sure his leaders didn't lose sight of bigger responsibilities such as taking care of employees, setting an example and accepting responsibility.

On Omaha Beach, Ruggero told stories illustrating principles of leadership, using Allied Commanding Gen. Dwight Eisenhower's rewriting his message accepting personal responsibility in the event the invasion failed. Then he got the executives to talk about people they've seen demonstrate similar courage on a smaller scale. The point was to get them to look at their own behavior and identify things to improve.

"We stood atop the remains of a German battery and I told them of the horrors that awaited the first wave of American boys who came ashore under fire," he recalled. "They saw their buddies die—calling for their mothers or praying the rosary. One soldier was wounded five times in one day.

"Lots of people today think the world is coming apart at the seams. In the face of all that there is to worry about, starting with terrorism and nuclear proliferation and ending who knows where, I choose to be optimistic. We'll get through somehow," he told Reuters.

Industry statistics side with Ruggero.

Business travel will increase 3.6 percent to 149 million trips in 2005, the Travel Industry Association says.

(November 2004)

"Reprinted with permission. All rights reserved. © Reuters 2004."

Part IX
Time Out

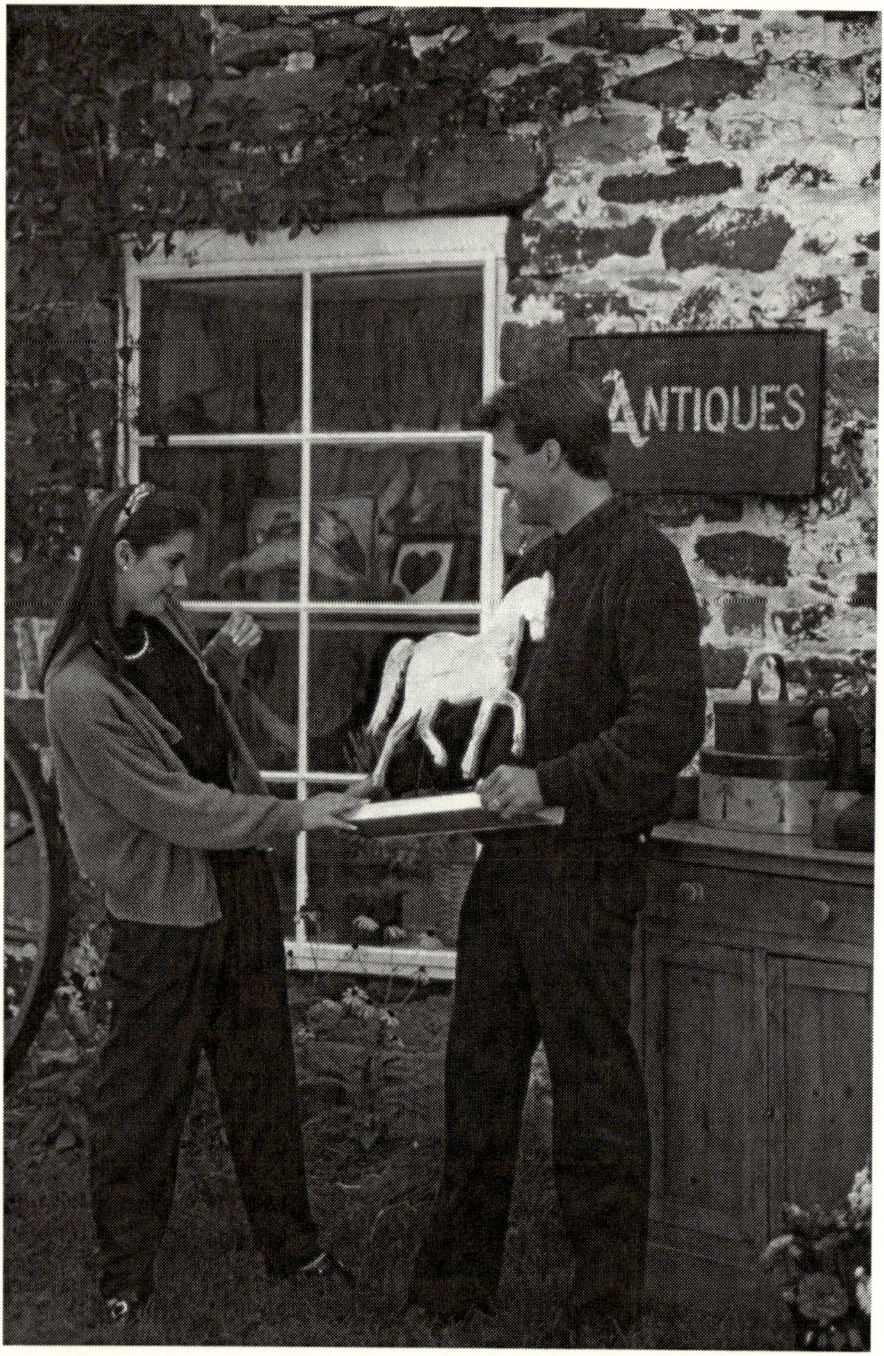
ANTIQUES

53

A World of Opportunities

As business travelers jet around the world collecting air miles and new cities, they have the opportunity to accumulate other things—from objects d'art to adventures to fresh acquaintances.

An antique Georgian carriage clock, elephant-back safari or a celebrity sighting can all make for fascinating conversation in the boardroom or at corporate social events.

It's good business sense for frequent travelers to remain open to any possibility to build contacts, broaden their knowledge, or learn how to spot a valuable investment.

Buying beautiful things during his world travels helps Claudio Zancani remember where he has been. The senior software executive for San Francisco-based Embarcadero Technologies, conducts business mainly in California and New York, but he has many reminders from past trips.

Zancani's job used to take him abroad 20 to 30 times a year to places such as England, Italy, Spain, Japan and South Korea. He rarely came back empty-handed.

"In Italy, I bought furniture for myself, and from Japan I brought back Samurai-type swords, paintings and teapots—some for me, some as presents for friends or colleagues," Zancani said. "Besides being beautiful, the objects are a reminder of where I've been and why people should travel."

Sharing Zancani's appreciation of what the world has to offer is London-based insurance executive John Trew. As a director of Britannia Ship Owners Insurance, he spent about three months of the year on the road, principally in India, Italy, the United States and Japan, where he purchased prints, woodcuts and other items for his home.

But his favorite place to shop is an international venue in his native England.

"The most recent thing I got was a sapphire and ruby ring for my wife at the last British Antique Dealers' Association Fair," Trew said.

The annual fair, featuring 100 dealers and items such as paintings, clocks, ceramics, textiles, jewelry and furniture, takes place in March in London's Chelsea district.

"Novices and collectors alike can learn from the experts, increase their knowledge of art and antiques and purchase something of enduring beauty and value," says Gillian Craig, the fair's organizer, who adds that antiques—such as, perhaps, a George IV wine funnel from 1827—are replacing the customary gold watch as a company reward for a job well done. "A fine antique or work of art as a corporate gift can send a message more eloquent than even the most luxurious gift from a high-profile retailer."

While picking up potential treasures can be an excellent investment, many other rewarding opportunities exist for globe-trotting executives.

- Business travelers to India can hone their boardroom jungle skills with the real thing—an educational Save the Tiger trip that takes them into the heart of tiger habitat. The annual trip has been led by veteran guide Brian Weirum, who developed the series for Mountain Travel Sobek (http://www.mtsobek.com), with profits donated to The Fund for the Tiger, a California-based nonprofit public charity that funds anti-poaching patrols.

- Conservation minded guests at Sun International hotels near the edge of Victoria Falls in Zambia, can go on an elephant-back safari along the Zambezi River in a national park.

"These adventures enhance the African experience and are very much in line with the conservation of wildlife and the environment," says Boris Bornman, general manager of Sun International's two-hotel resort.

- Ecology-conscious travelers heading for South America might choose to stay at a place such as the Kapawi EcoLodge and Reserve, in the Ecuadorean Amazon. The state-of-the-art project was built in partnership with the indigenous Achuar Indians and without the use of a single metal nail. Selected by a panel of global environmentalists, it was awarded the first annual Skal International Eco Tourism Award.

- Described as a "natural hunting ground for interior decorators, collectors and museum curators" London's Spring Fine Art & Antiques Fair at Olympia offers visitors the chance to "bag" a 9-foot crocodile made from bottle tops by South African artist Robert Barley, a 17th-Century Portuguese silk bedspread, or a pair of 18th Century Chinese palace doors with massive iron handles. (http://www.olympia-antiques.com)

- In the celebrity-studded urban jungles of New York City, the Showbiz Insiders Tour is the first to take visitors behind the scenes of hit television and Broadway productions, allowing them to meet Broadway actors or go backstage.

"It gives an insider's perspective through the heart of New York City entertainment giants and a glimpse at the magic of stage and screen," says Tom Lewis, president of Gray Line New York Sightseeing. (http://www.NewYorkSightseeing.com)

(January 2003)

"Reprinted with permission. All rights reserved. © Reuters 2003."

54

Navigating the Euro Zone

The introduction of the euro as the single currency for 300 million Europeans was also the signal for an early spring cleaning for millions of American travelers—time to turn pockets inside out and empty desk drawers, envelopes and jam jars of foreign money that had accumulated from trips taken abroad over the years.

While numismatists and sentimental souvenir hounds might have viewed it as an opportunity to order "beautifully mounted" sets of the newly-defunct currencies of 12 of the 15 European Union countries, business travelers were looking for a means to dispose of their own personal "collections."

At American Express in New York, a spokesperson urged "everyone to find all those francs, D-marks and guilder notes ... and bring them in for conversion."

Thomas Cook's David Montgomery, vice president for retail foreign exchange, agreed that "sooner rather than later" is better for converting the currencies, but "we anticipate still buying them for a considerable period of time. The deadlines in each of the euro countries only refer to how long the national currencies can be used in stores and restaurants ... it doesn't mean they are worthless. At some central banks, the deadline stretches until 2012."

Undoubtedly, Americans doing business overseas will find their lives greatly simplified by what was being called the biggest monetary changeover in history.

Andrea Sertoli, president of Chicago-based Select Italy (www.selectitaly.com), a customized travel service for discerning clients, suggested taking the European currencies along and converting them locally. "The others can go to their local U.S. bank, though they shouldn't expect favorable exchange rates, or they can check with central banks if they are planning to travel to Europe."

Waxing sentimental on the demise of the lira was Italian-born John Buzzetta, president of Van Zandt Newspapers, LLC in East Texas: "There are things I'll miss about it—such as feeling rich, with lots of money in my pocket. In Florence, a gelato was 10,000 lire, and a two-night stay at a hotel was more than one million lire." On the other hand, "I won't miss having a fistful of coins that amounted only to about 90 cents."

"Although it's nice to see a unified monetary system for most of Western Europe, I hope this is not the beginning of more homogenization. I hope each country maintains its diversity in food, culture, language and shopping. It's scary to think of Europe as the same vast blandness of fast foods, franchises and shopping strips that we have in the United States," Buzzetta said.

One international business consultant is hoping the changeover will bring him multiple rewards.

"I plan to keep all the coins and bills I have as they will eventually be useful heirlooms, or collector's items to sell," said John Freivalds, president of JFA Marketing (www.jfamarketing.com) in Lexington, Virginia. In 1996, he devised a "Periodic Table of Money" poster that became popular with corporations, global travel services and schools. He was planning to revive the poster—which shows currencies from around the world, their proper name and slang name–and use it as "a transition tool."

In Los Angeles, public relations executive Kirsten Schmidt, a native of Germany, says she has the best of both worlds.

"My German friends and I certainly have discussed this topic. Luckily, my mother-in-law who visited from Germany for the holidays will take my remaining 412 deutschmarks back with her, exchange them for me, and bring the equivalent euro amount with her on her next trip to Los Angeles this spring," said Schmidt, the U.S. director for Berlin Tourismus Marketing.

"Coins from other European countries that I had collected in numerous envelopes, will be welcomed as play money for my children," she said.

In the short term, the money swap was a bonanza for charities, who cashed in from the largesse of travelers wanting to benefit a good cause, while at the same time ridding themselves of unwanted cash.

In the longer term, however, some expressed concern that organizations like the United Nations Children's Fund (UNICEF) might feel a negative impact since air passengers won't have as many leftover coins to donate in envelopes on their flights home.

Pockets full of change have never been an issue for Jean-Jacques Pergant, general manager of The Berkeley hotel in London's elegant Belgravia section.

"I can't say that I have a lot of coins stashed in a drawer simply because I have managed, so far, to utilize them and have often used the British Airways (Change for Good) idea of turning them in for charity," Pergant said.

For those with big dreams of making a mint off their travel mementos, Beth Deisher, editor of Coin World, a guide for collectors, investors and enthusiasts, has some down-to-earth advice:

"You have to remember that most of these coins are relatively common and have been in circulation and are not in the highest state of preservation that collectors would want. It also depends on how many are turned in to get melted down. In two or three years we'll have a better take on that," Deisher said. "In the meantime, they make nice souvenirs of a trip or starter sets for future collectors. But as far as investment ... you're looking at 75 to 100 years."

(January 2002)

"Reprinted with permission. All rights reserved. © Reuters 2002."

55

Armchair Travel for Idle Dynamos

As business travel slows to a crawl over the holidays, many harried executives accustomed to a hectic pace of shuttling between cities and airports feel welcome relief. But others may find the lull unsettling and, like an addict, experience withdrawal symptoms.

It's a good time, says Dr. Anie Kalaygian, for stressed-out travelers to re-evaluate and try to shift the emphasis of their lives—perhaps by getting lost in a book.

"The degree of discomfort forced idleness brings to individuals depends on what meaning they attach to that part of their life," Kalaygian, a clinical psychologist and professor of psychology at Fordham University in New York, said. "Is work their passion, their way of survival, contribution to society, or a bit of everything?"

From the three aspects of life—having, being and connecting–she said many people put material possessions first.

Lorna Kelly, the first female Fine Art auctioneer at Sotheby's in New York, was leading a glamorous, high-powered life. Then a friend gave her a book about Mother Teresa, which led her to the sweltering slums of Calcutta. The fashionable, statuesque blonde Kelly arrived in India wearing designer clothes and bright red nail polish to care for the poorest of the poor as a volunteer for the Missionaries of Charity.

Out of that experience came Kelly's own self-published book, "The Camel Knows the Way," detailing her journey from an English Catholic girls school to life in New York, divorce, alcoholism and the spiritual quest that led to a friendship with Mother Teresa herself.

Kelly was invited to Rome as a witness for Mother Teresa's beatification, and now auctions at charity events.

People who are too attached to their jobs "feel useless when they are not contributing. There is a tremendous emptiness," Kalaygian said. Some suddenly idle travelers find it so hard to give up work that they have dreams about flying, or wake in a panic thinking they forgot their passport.

For them, reading a book that helps maintain their competitive edge may help fill the vacuum. "The Myth of Homeland Security," by security expert Marcus J. Ranum, deals with how much can or cannot be controlled. The chapters on "Airline Insecurity" and "The Business of Computer Security" may be especially useful for frequent travelers.

Corporate executives who, like armies, travel on their stomachs, will find practical application in "The New York Restaurant Cookbook" (Rizzoli International Publications), a book designed to win the hearts, minds and stomachs of world travelers.

Author Florence Fabricant goes into the kitchens and dining rooms of 115 restaurants in the city that "offers the most internationally diverse dining experiences of any city in the world," says Cristyne L. Nicholas, CEO of NYC & Company (www.nycvisit.com), a nonprofit group that promotes New York tourism worldwide.

Included are recipes from some of the restaurant menus—from the Second Avenue Deli's Chicken Soup to Nobu's Black Cod With Miso to Payard Bistro's Bittersweet Chocolate Souffle—which Fabricant, a food writer, has adapted for home cooks.

Losing touch with the little things in life is easy for highly mobile executives who have a lot of responsibility. Books about people, their roots and childhood memories allow armchair travelers to "connect with the fabric of humanity," said Kalaygian, who also recommends taking notes.

In "A Long Way from Home," (Random House) broadcast journalist Tom Brokaw looks back at growing up in the American Heartland in the 1940s and '50s. He lauds the importance of having been instilled with wholesome values like hard work, self reliance and decency, which in today's world are viewed by some as embarrassingly old-fashioned.

Another book inspired by childhood memories, "Neither East Nor West" (Washington Square Press), crosses the cultural divide with style and sensitivity. Author Christiane Bird, a New Yorker whose physician father was doing volunteer work in Iran, tells a compelling personal story that is particularly relevant in light of today's turmoil in the Middle East.

Animal lovers will empathize with Peter Gethers as he pays tribute to his pet, arguably the world's most well-traveled, socially sought-after cat—Norton the Scottish Fold, aka "The Cat Who Went to Paris" and "A Cat Abroad."

The last journey of Gethers' beloved feline, whose obituary appeared in the New York Times and whose passing was noted by Time magazine, is lovingly documented by his owner "blubbering through the whole process" in "The Cat Who'll Live Forever" (Broadway Books).

Life without books would indeed be "very minimal," said Lorna Kelly, for whom reading is as much a passion as working. "It's something I do as an activity, on a par with the gym or running around the reservoir. It's a choice I make. Will I spend time on the phone, go see a movie or finish the book? It all depends what's important in life to you."

(January 2004)

"Reprinted with permission. All rights reserved. © Reuters 2004."

About the Author

Photo by David Beyda

Gunna Dickson started traveling when she was 7 months old. She has been a working journalist for more than 20 years. As a New York-based writer/sub-editor at Reuters international wire service, she has been published in the United States, Canada, Europe, Asia, South America, South Africa and Australia. Her work has been translated online into French, Spanish, German, Korean, Arabic and Russian and appeared regularly on Web sites such as Yahoo, MSNBC, CNN, Washington Post, Boston Globe, St. Louis Post Dispatch, USA Today, Forbes and NYT.com.

While Travel Editor at The New York Daily News, she contributed the New York and Long Island chapters for UK's Thomas Cook Touring Handbook series (1996) "On the Road Around New England" fly-drive guide. In 2006, she translated a World War II memoir, "The Red Fog."

A member of New York Travel Writers Association and The Foreign Press Association, she is the winner of two Front Page awards (2002 and 2003) from the Newswomen's Club of New York.

Raised bi-lingual (English-Latvian) in the United States, she has lived in Germany, France and Denmark, and traveled extensively.

978-0-595-42378-1
0-595-42378-7

Printed in the United States
71492LV00002B/76-114